NATIONAL PARKS OF THE WEST

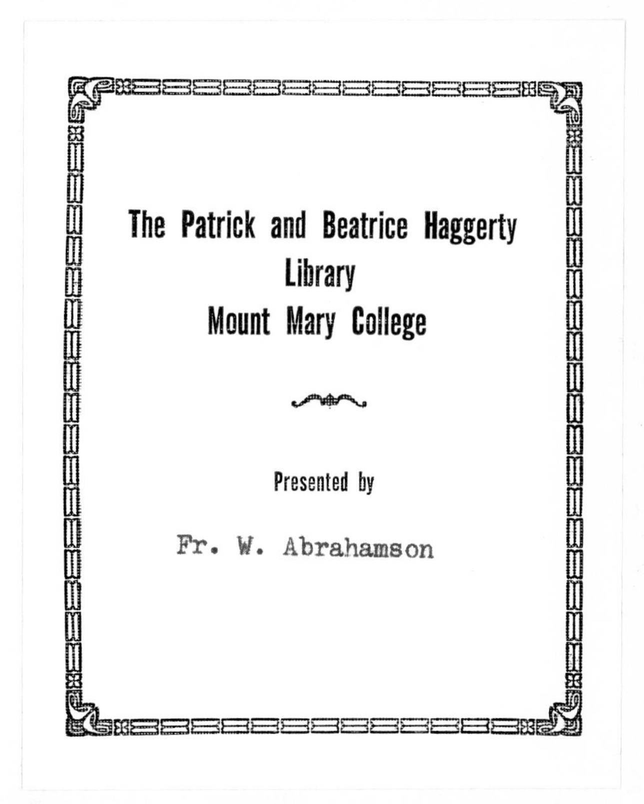

NATIONAL PARKS of the WEST

By the Editors of Sunset Books
and Sunset Magazine

Lane Publishing Co.
Menlo Park, California

EDITED BY: DOROTHY N. KRELL

BOOK DESIGN: JOE SENEY

MAPS: JAMES M. CUTTER, ANDY SAPORITO, ELLS MARUGG

ILLUSTRATIONS: EARL THOLLANDER, E. D. BILLS

Editor, Sunset Books: David E. Clark

First Printing May 1980

Library of Congress No. 79-90339. ISBN 0-376-05583-9. Lithographed in United States.

Front Cover: Grand Teton National Park, by Russell Lamb.
Back Cover: Grand Canyon National Park, by Josef Muench.
Title Page: Yellowstone National Park, by Steven Fuller.

PREFACE

THIS BOOK IS A PICTORIAL INTERPRETATION of the national parks in the West, the score of scenic preserves whose very names are household synonyms for spectacular beauty—Yellowstone, Yosemite, Grand Canyon, Zion, Mount McKinley, Olympic—parks that encompass within their 12 million acres most of the nation's finest mountain and desert scenery.

As its title indicates, this is a book about *national parks*, which are defined as areas of outstanding scenic beauty that have been set aside by Congress to be preserved in their natural state for the benefit and enjoyment of the people. Although some *national monuments* partially meet this definition, we have reluctantly, for lack of space, confined our main coverage to the areas officially designated as national parks. National monuments, along with national recreation areas, historic sites, memorials, and the West's one national seashore, are described briefly in a special section beginning on page 250. There are 93 within the geographic scope of this book—the area from the Rocky Mountains west to the Hawaiian Islands.

This edition is a third look at the subject of the West's national parks. Innumerable changes have taken place within the parks in the 15 years since this book was first published. New roads have been built, old routes realigned, and miles of trails added. Off-season facilities have been developed, concessioners have upgraded and expanded their facilities, and, most important, Congress has added five new Western parks to the roster.

We wish to acknowledge the contribution made by Paul C. Johnson, editor of the original edition of this book. Much of his research has been retained in material in this new version and in the second edition edited by Jack McDowell.

We also wish to acknowledge with appreciation the excellent cooperation that we received from the concessioners and from the National Park Service, from Washington down to the individual parks, in the supplying and checking of technical information for this book. We would like to thank particularly the superintendents and ranger naturalists who worked with us.

Our pictorial interpretation of the parks is offered with the wish that it may partly accomplish what John Muir hoped his own book on the national parks would do when it was published in 1898. Like Muir, we have tried "to show forth the beauty, grandeur, and all-embracing usefulness of our wild mountain forest reservations and parks, with a view to inciting people to come and enjoy them, and get them into their hearts, that so at length their preservation and right use might be made sure of."

ALASKA

MT. McKINLEY

BEAUTY, GRANDEUR...USEFULNESS

WEST OF THE CONTINENTAL DIVIDE lie millions of acres of the nation's scenic superlatives—the deepest canyons, highest waterfalls, tallest peaks, and biggest trees. Mountain ranges pierce the clouds; crystal clear lakes are stirred by gentle breezes; mists swirl through cathedral-like rain forests; waves break on pristine shores. Protected here are the habitats of an incredible variety of wildlife. Wilderness areas challenge men's spirits. In developed areas of the parks, museums, visitor centers, naturalist programs, and trailside exhibits promote understanding of the natural wonders that exist here. This map shows the general location of these national parks that encompass the most majestic country in the West (Alaska and the Hawaiian Islands are shown but are distorted both in scale and position).

HAWAIIAN ISLANDS

HALEAKALA

HAWAII VOLCANOES

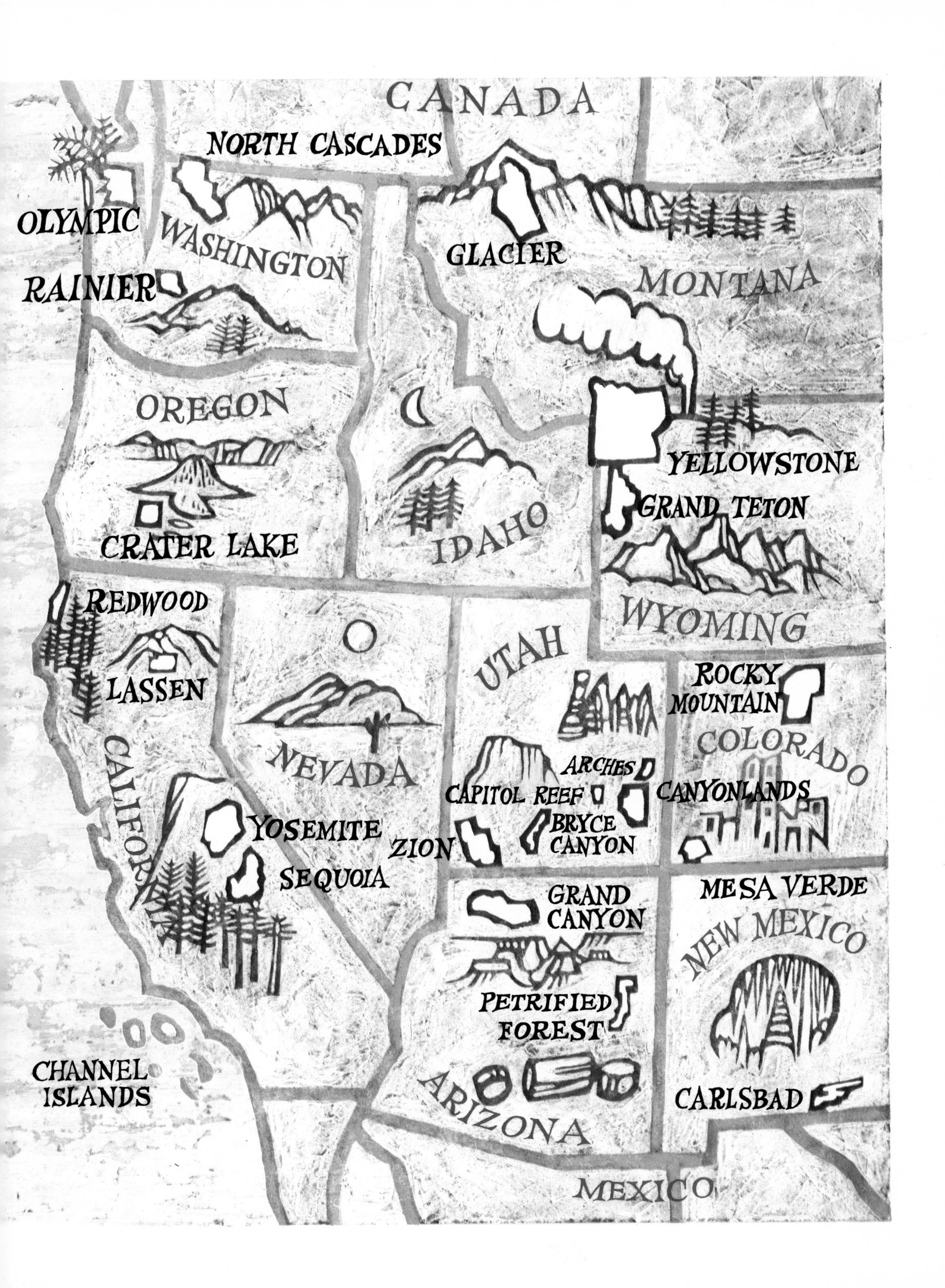
CANADA
NORTH CASCADES
OLYMPIC
WASHINGTON
RAINIER
GLACIER
MONTANA
OREGON
CRATER LAKE
IDAHO
YELLOWSTONE
GRAND TETON
WYOMING
REDWOOD
LASSEN
NEVADA
UTAH
ROCKY MOUNTAIN
COLORADO
CALIFORNIA
ARCHES
CAPITOL REEF
CANYONLANDS
YOSEMITE
BRYCE CANYON
ZION
SEQUOIA
GRAND CANYON
MESA VERDE
NEW MEXICO
PETRIFIED FOREST
CHANNEL ISLANDS
ARIZONA
CARLSBAD
MEXICO

CONTENTS

THE NATIONAL PARK IDEA

"THOUSANDS OF TIRED, NERVE-SHAKEN, OVER-CIVILIZED people are beginning to find out that going to the mountains is going home; that wildness is a necessity; and that mountain parks and reservations are useful not only as fountains of timber and irrigating rivers, but as fountains of life." So wrote John Muir, naturalist, conservationist, and pioneer spokesman for the national parks.

When Muir expressed these sentiments, the year was 1898. There were only four national parks in existence—three of them in California—and they could be reached only by an endless stage ride over backbreaking roads. The fact that thousands were making this arduous trip is an indication of the depth of the need that was felt even then to "go home to the mountains."

What Muir sensed as a significant truth then is even more cogent today, as 32 million visitors converge each year on the Western national parks, seeking spiritual and physical renewal and the reassurance of contact, however brief and communal, with nature.

Westerners are fortunate to have within their domain the lion's share of the nation's spectacular scenery, and most of it is contained within the boundaries of the national parks lying west of the Continental Divide. Here, held in trust for the country as a whole are a dozen scenic superlatives—the deepest canyons, highest waterfalls, tallest peaks, and biggest trees in the nation. Here the traveler can stand witness to the awesome forces of earthbuilding: the power of running water or grinding ice to shape the surface of the earth; the restlessness pent up within the planet, revealed in fire-fountains of lava or spouting columns of steam. He can observe the grand cycle of life, seen in the wash of spring wildflowers, the frolicking bear cubs, or the golden fires of October aspen. In a few weeks' travel, a vacationer can see perpetual snow and active glaciers, petrified forests and mountains of glass; he can follow a trail through a wild-flower park, watch armies of elk on the move, or walk through a dead city that was a vital community 1,500 years before Plymouth Rock. Within the parks, motorists can drive over the spine of a continent, and hikers can safely roam for weeks in a primeval wilderness, unchanged from the days of the cavemen.

To devotees of the national parks, it is often things subtler than geysers, fumaroles, and the riven earth that bring them back vacation after vacation. To the camper, it is the camaraderie of the campfire or the trail; to the fisherman the park is a place where time stands still while he trolls a lake or casts into a rushing stream. To families it is a place where the flash of wonder and delight glows on the faces of their children when they first feel a running stream against their shins, or see a fawn, a thieving jay or chipmunk, or a bear in all his natural majesty. To some, it is a garden of trees and wildflowers, stones and lichens; an aviary; and a place to watch animals going about their daily chores. To all, the parks offer the soul-stretching experience of being alone in a world of wide-open space, of grand vistas of forest and mountain and great storms rumbling across the land. The experience is remembered for the tang of fresh mountain air, the blessing of pure silence, the benediction of alpenglow. In short, the parks offer a return to nature, and the renewal that comes from re-contact with a wild and primitive environment.

To make sure that all who want to enjoy the parks can do so, at whatever level of experience, is the dedicated mission of the National Park Service.

The seed of the national park idea was planted more than a century ago in California, where commercial exploitation of Yosemite Valley and the senseless cutting of giant sequoias had aroused great public concern. A handful of men banded together to put pressure on Congress to preserve the beautiful valley and a grove of the irreplaceable trees, both of which were on federal property. With little debate, a law was passed in 1864 and signed by President Lincoln, then in the heat of the Civil War, that granted Yosemite Valley and the Mariposa Grove of Big Trees to the state of California. This was the first time that any government anywhere had set aside public lands purely for the preservation of scenic values, and, as such, the law was a landmark in conservation.

The portion of Yosemite turned over to the state was only a 10-square-mile strip that included the famous valley and a square mile of trees 35 miles to the south. In size, it was far from the huge park of today. Furthermore, as a grant to a state, this was not a "national" park in today's meaning of the term, but a state park. The first true national park was created in Yellowstone eight years later, and it is from it that the National Park Service dates its official beginning.

The idea for a national park was first presented before an historic campfire in 1870 by a Montana attorney named Cornelius Hedges. He was a member of a famous exploring party known as the Washburn-Langford-Doane expedition that surveyed the wonders of Yellowstone (see page 197) with the purpose of puncturing or confirming the incredible rumors then circulating about the thermal spectacles in the area.

After exploring the region for more than a month, on their last night before returning home, the party held a campfire meeting at the junction of three rivers in western Yellowstone. Under the laws of the day, all were entitled to stake claims on the land and its geysers. As the men were discussing how they would divide this wonderland among themselves, Hedges made a far-reaching proposal. Turning the conversation away from private gain, he eloquently proposed that they work for the preservation of the whole area under government protection. The men enthusiastically endorsed the idea (all but one hold-out), and after their return, several of them campaigned for a law to set aside the area. So effective was their presentation that Congress passed the necessary legislation only 17

NATIONAL PARK SERVICE

TWO GREAT CONSERVATIONISTS, *President Theodore Roosevelt and John Muir, stand on Glacier Point in Yosemite, where they camped together for five days in 1903. As a result of this meeting, Roosevelt returned to Washington determined to expand the federal protection of the nation's scenic, historic, and natural heritage. In the next few years, he brought protection to several million acres by proclaiming national monuments.*

months after the expedition's return, thus creating the first, and as far as anyone then knew the last, national park.

The law, based in part on the earlier legislation that had created the Yosemite Grant, set forth principles that have been followed with some modifications for a century. Under this legislative mandate, the National Park Service is charged with a dual responsibility: (a) to preserve for all time the natural wonders within its boundaries in an undisturbed state and (b) to make them available for the enjoyment of all the people.

Under its commitment to preserve the parks in their natural state, the Park Service is required to protect wildlife from trappers and hunters and to preserve the forests, streams, and lakes from despoliation. Thus, timber cutting is prohibited and trees are left to topple of old age or to be blown down in a windstorm. Once fallen, they are left where they fell. Mining and extraction of petroleum are forbidden, and so is the grazing of sheep and cattle. Private cabins cannot be built within a national park, and the only structures permitted are those needed by government services and the concessioners.

Preservation of the natural scene by the Park Service so that all the people may enjoy it often calls for skillful balancing of opposing needs.

Under its charter, the Park Service must welcome all who wish to come to the parks. With improved roads and the proliferation of the automobile, the parks have become more accessible to more people each year, and crowded conditions prevail in seasons of heavy tourist travel. The visitors head instinctively for the centers of popular interest, thereby compounding congestion. Although the Park Service tries to interest tourists in outlying areas and encourages off-season visits, these measures do not solve the problem. Crowding increases each year, threatening to submerge the parks, scenic wonders and all.

And what of the future? Tradition and legal precedent do not guarantee that the natural parks can be kept to their dedicated mission without vigilant adherence to the policies under which they are operated.

It is theoretically possible to create a new national park anywhere within the federal domain today, but in areas containing mineral deposits, harvestable timber, dam sites, or grazing land, opposition is almost inevitable. One of the newest parks, Canyonlands, located in a mineral-rich area of Utah, was long a subject of controversy and was much shrunk in size from earlier proposals when it was finally approved. And it is not surprising that national parks recently established in Washington's North Cascades and in California's coast-redwood belt were vigorously opposed, not only by timber industry advocates but by spokesmen for communities dependent on the lumbering industry. As this book goes to press, critical decisions are still to be made regarding the Channel Islands off California's coast (pages 106-109) and several wilderness areas in Alaska (pages 232-235). These areas consist of a variety of delicately balanced ecosystems which may easily be irreparably damaged. Legislation has been introduced to officially change their designations from that of national monuments to national parks.

For that matter, long-established parks are never completely immune from forays by mineral, water, and recreational interests seeking to exploit the public domain. The constituted agencies are sometimes ill equipped to repel invaders because of red tape, interservice rivalries, or local pressures, and occasionally have to rely on bolstering from the outside to protect the public's scenic heritage. Conservationists have leaped to the barricade several times in recent years and their task forces are on permanent alert. In the forefront of the defending forces, the bristly Sierra Club has employed every strategem—court injunctions, lawsuits, advertising campaigns—to keep parklands inviolate. The club has fought to prevent Grand Canyon from being dammed into a lake, to block highway engineers from bulldozing a swath through public groves of redwoods, to stop developers from cutting a highway through Sequoia National Park. Conservationists win some of the battles, compromise most of them, and lose a few. But the struggle continues for the protectors both within and outside the guardian agencies, for there will always be men who can see trees only as lumber, rivers as sources of energy, canyons as reservoirs, and mountain meadows as grazing land for cattle, heedless of the broader values of the natural landscape to the nation as a whole.

NORTH CASCADES

AMERICA'S ALPINE WILDERNESS

PARK FACTS: *Location:* North central Washington. *Discovered:* 1792. *Established:* October 2, 1968. *Size:* 1,053 sq. mi. (including Ross Lake and Lake Chelan national recreation areas). *Altitude:* Sea level to 9,000 ft. *Climate:* Cool and damp on west side of Cascades; warm days, cool nights on east side. *Season:* Early April to mid-October; high country, mid-July to mid-September. *Annual visitors:* 931,500. *Accommodations:* Campgrounds (no trailer hookups). *Activities:* Hiking, mountaineering, boating, cross-country skiing. *Information:* Supt., North Cascades Park, Sedro Woolley, WA 98284.

A LAND FOR MOUNTAINEERS, North Cascades best reveals its grandeur to those who frequent its hiking or riding trails. The park, as established in 1968 after thirty years of agitation, is portioned into four units: two wilderness areas (North and South units) and Ross Lake and Lake Chelan recreational areas (see map on page 16). Visitors can traverse the park by a single east-west highway, but the two large wilderness units divided by the highway corridor are essentially backcountry. The perimeters of the park are accessible by boat from Lake Chelan or Ross Lake in the adjacent recreation areas.

A few miles of resolute trudging brings spectacular individual rewards. Everywhere is the looming presence of the mountains, with soaring glacier-burdened peaks, cloud-piercing needle spires, flower-starred ridgetop meadows, clumps of alpine fir, and views down steep heather slopes to mounded gray moraines and the deep, wooded, glacial valleys beyond. There are the deep crackling sounds of sloughing ice and tumbling avalanches when the day is warm, and of thunder when it is stormy; and always there is a background roar of falling water, sometimes muted by distance, sometimes lost in the rush of the wind, accented by the chirp of a pika, or accompanied by the summery hum of a fly.

For travelers who are not inured to the damp weather of northern Washington, a trip into this realm can have its disappointments. Summer weather on the western slopes is normally wet—meaning rain, hail, snow, sleet, envelopment in dripping clouds, or simply the lingering presence of leaden overcast that keeps wet things (including the hiker himself) from drying out. Often, vacationers in the park will sense rather than see the surrounding mountains from one day to the next. However, experienced hikers equip themselves with appropriate rain gear and tolerate the drizzle in the knowledge that sooner or later the mist will clear and reveal the all-encompassing spectacles of peak, glacier, and forest under a sparkling sun.

PRINCIPAL BEACON OF THE PARK, *Mount Shuksan, reflected here in Price Lake, rises above its glaciers to 9,131 feet. Unlike other major peaks in the Cascades, Shuksan is non-volcanic in origin. A trail leads to its ice-crowned summit.*

DAVID MUENCH

KEITH GUNNAR

GATEWAY TO HIKING TRAILS in the park, Ross Lake is part of the North Cascades complex of park and recreation area lands. Access is by unimproved road from Canada or trail from Diablo Lake. A resort at the south end offers rental boats and water taxi service.

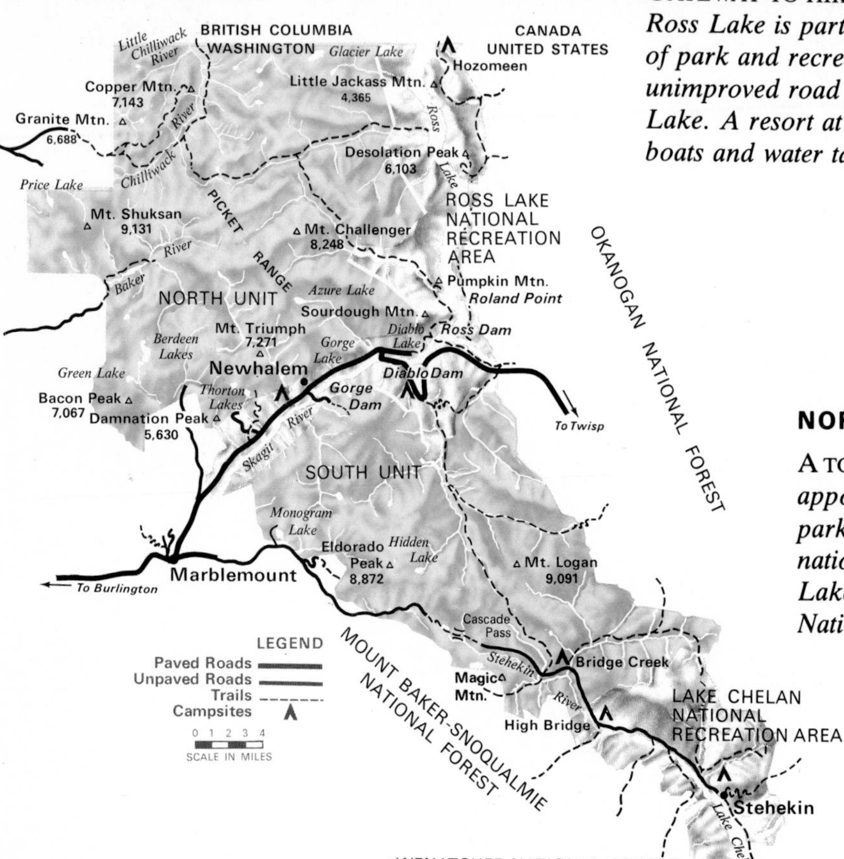

NORTH CASCADES NATIONAL PARK

A TOPOGRAPHIC JUMBLE, the park is apportioned into four units: two units of the park (North Unit and South Unit) and two national recreation areas (Ross Lake and Lake Chelan), all administered by the National Park Service.

ED COOPER

ALDER GROVES *flourish at low elevations. As the auto route that divides the park's North and South units climbs higher, the landscape changes to forests of fir, pine, larch, and hemlock, flowered meadows, and windy passes.*

PHILIP HYDE

IN LATE JULY, *wildflowers color the ridgetop meadows near Cascade Pass, a favorite hiking area. From west to east, the plant communities in the park range from rain forest through subalpine coniferous, verdant meadow, and alpine tundra back down to pine forests and sunny, dry shrublands.*

RUSSELL LAMB

RAYS OF A LATE AFTERNOON SUN *filter through the clouds in this view from just below Magic Mountain, which straddles the boundary of the park's South Unit.*

OLYMPIC

THREE GREAT PARKS IN ONE

PARK FACTS: *Location:* Olympic Peninsula, northwestern Washington. *Discovered:* 1774. *Established:* June 29, 1938. *Size:* 1,420 sq. mi. *Altitude:* Sea level to 7,965 ft. *Climate:* Summers cool and sunny, but rain likely; winters wettest in the conterminous United States. *Season:* All year, but some main roads closed by snow. *Annual visitors:* 2,997,000. *Accommodations:* Lodges, cabins, campgrounds, trailer parks. *Activities:* Hiking, boating (Lake Crescent), ice climbing, cross-country skiing (Hurricane Ridge). *Information:* Supt., Olympic National Park, 600 E. Park Ave., Port Angeles, WA 98362.

OF ALL THE NATIONAL PARKS, THE MOST DIVERSIFIED in character and climate is Olympic. Here you will find seacoast and mountain peak, rain forest and glacier, and an unbelievably abrupt change of weather patterns. The western side of the park has the wettest winter climate in the United States, with nearly *12 feet* of precipitation annually. The eastern side is the driest part of the Pacific Coast outside of Southern California.

Located on the Olympic Peninsula in the extreme northwest corner of Washington, the park contains one of the last virgin wilderness areas between Mexico and Canada. Through it wind hundreds of miles of hiking and horseback trails. Along the trails, as welcome retreats in case of sudden storm or the arrival of darkness, are many simple overnight shelters.

The Olympic Mountains are centered on the peninsula between the Pacific Ocean to the west and Hood Canal to the east. The land rises gently from the water and suddenly steepens, culminating in the heights of Mount Olympus. In comparison with the altitudes of inland mountains, the summit of Olympus—7,965 feet—and those of other peaks above 7,000 feet do not sound impressive. But this range rises from sea level, and it is massive. Jagged peaks shade the deep canyons, about 60 glaciers lie in the cirques, and shaggy forests climb from the sea up to timberline.

The rain forests are the strangest portions of the park, and to many the most fascinating. Their vegetation is as luxuriant as that of the Amazon jungles. Great ferns spring from beds of thick moss. Thickets of vine maple lend mystery, and gigantic trees trail heavy draperies of moss that filter the sunlight to an eerie yellow-green. There are three such forests—in the valleys of the rivers

AVALANCHE LILIES *burst into bloom while snow still lingers in this meadow at Hurricane Ridge. A white-capped Bailey Range looms on the horizon southwest of the ridge.*

DARWIN VAN CAMPEN

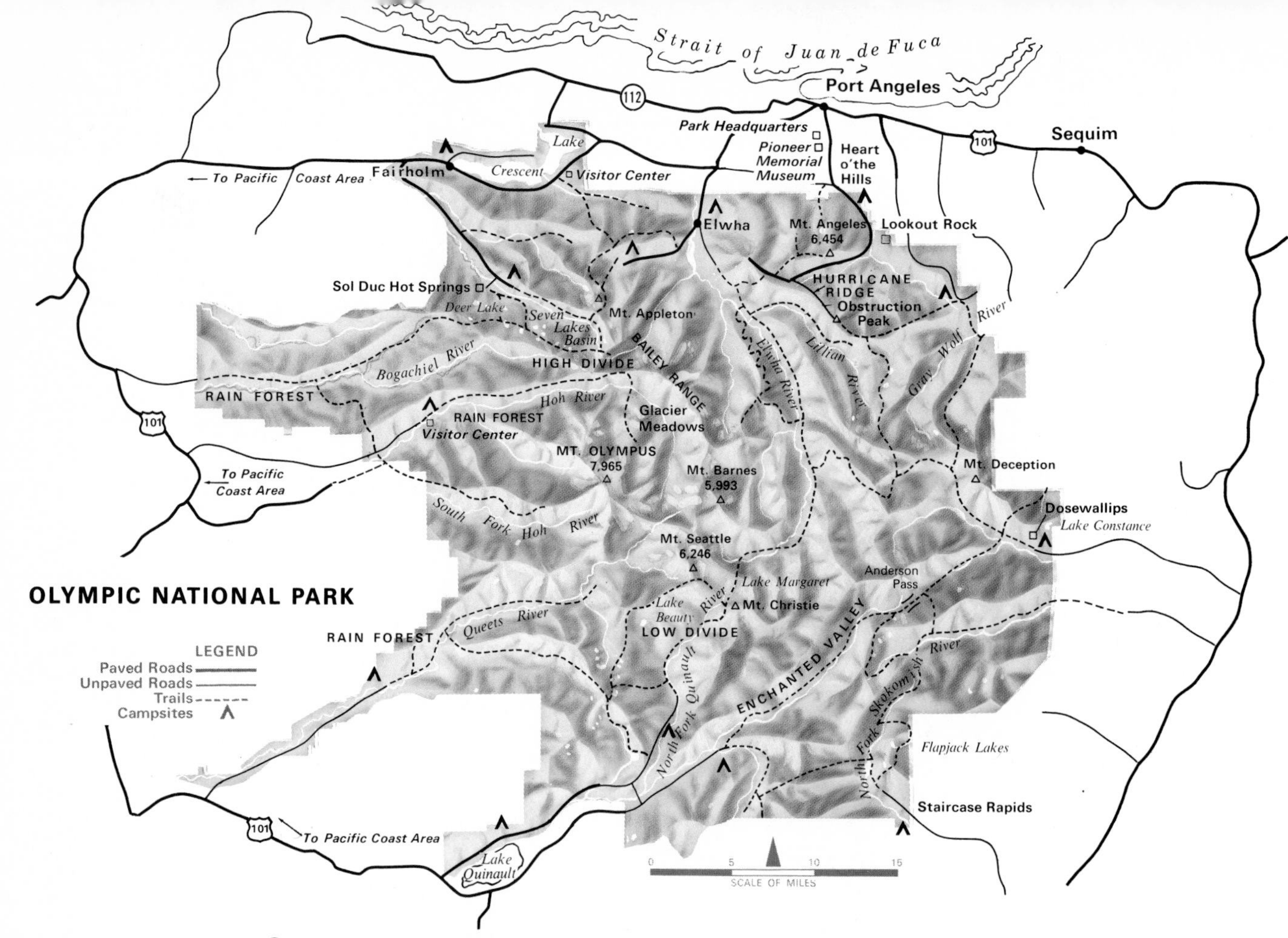

OLYMPIC NATIONAL PARK *is divided into two parts: a thin coastal strip (map on page 28) and an inland block. Roads connect the two sections, but the park boundaries do not surround both. Most of the main body of the park is up-and-down country, a confusing mass of mountains and canyons.*

KEITH GUNNAR

FLOATING LEISURELY *down the upper Queets River, you'll have time to fish, swim, and look for wildlife—or simply relax and enjoy the superb scenery. An unpaved road follows the river from Highway 101, ending at Queets Campground—a good place to launch your raft or boat and also a starting point for high-country trails in the park.*

Hoh, Queets, and Quinault—and in them are found several of the world's largest specimens of luxuriant plant life.

About five thousand Olympic elk dwell in the park. Blacktail deer live here, and so do black bears and a host of smaller animals.

Like a few other national parks, Olympic is a land of water, and it boasts not only lakes and rivers but the ocean as well. To preserve the rugged beauty of unmodified coastline with jagged cliffs, islands, and coves, the park takes in 50 miles of shoreline, perhaps the most primitive remaining in this country.

Along with hiking, mountain climbing attracts many to Olympic. Many of the lesser peaks can be conquered in safety by the inexperienced, but the more difficult demand skill. Once attained, the heights offer views that are all-embracing—peaks on every side, snow and ice, flower-strewn meadows, and the heavy coniferous forest. Beyond are the waters of the Pacific, Strait of Juan de Fuca, and Puget Sound, and the cities and towns of northwest Washington.

No trip to this peninsula would be complete without a visit to the Indian fishing village of La Push, at the mouth of Quillayute River on the ocean strip. Here fishermen still use dugout canoes and dip nets to take silversmelt in spring.

OLYMPIC HAS HAD A LONG AND EMBATTLED HISTORY. Over a span of 40 argumentative years, it has been set up in turn as a forest preserve (1897-1906), a national monument (1906-33), and, finally, a national park (1938). It has been shifted back and forth between the Department of Interior (1897-1905, 1933 to date) and the Department of Agriculture (1905-1933), and it has ranged in size from an initial 615,000 acres, down to a low in 1915 of 300,000 acres, and back up to its present size, 908,692 acres. Its boundaries have been adjusted a half dozen times.

Principal reason for this checkered history has been strong local opposition to the park built on the conviction that it would withdraw thousands of acres of harvestable timber needed to sustain the state's giant lumbering industry. First moves to set aside the area were introduced in the 1890s, and though repeated attempts were made in later years, including a bill in 1905 to establish it as Elk National Park, the park was not created until 1938. The protracted battling surged in and out of congressional committee hearings, reached into the President's Cabinet, and even drew President Franklin Roosevelt to Port Angeles in an attempt to compromise the disputed issues. In time, proponents of the park were able to win their point that creation of the national park would bring long-run benefits to the state, as well as the nation, that would greatly outweigh the short-run benefits to be derived from logging off the trees, and the park was finally legislated into existence.

The name chosen for the park harks back to an English sea captain, John Mears, who sighted the high mountains from the coast in 1788 and named the highest peak Mount Olympus, believing it deserved the dignity of association with the Greek home of the gods. For 24 years, Olympic was known as Mount Olympus National Monument, and the park was very nearly named Mount Olympus National Park when it was established.

KEITH GUNNAR

LIFE CYCLE OF A RAIN FOREST: *After a tree topples, it becomes a nurse log for new seedlings. Bacteria and fungi slowly break down its fibers, mosses and lichens cover it, giving a surface in which tree seeds germinate and sprout; a seedling takes root; and in time a new tree grows.*

THE GOING IS MADE EASIER *by this log trail through a boggy section of the Elwha Valley. Campgrounds here are trailheads for high-country hikers. Although three-fourths of Olympic's precipitation falls between October and March, hikers in the park should be prepared for unpredictable weather at any time of year.*

KEITH GUNNAR

Rain Forest

THE LUMINOUS WORLD OF THE RAIN FOREST is filled with a soft green light reflected and refracted by the mosses and the translucent maple leaves. To a well-traveled visitor, there are no strange or unknown organisms. Everything that grows in the rain forest, except the Sitka spruce, grows in other places. The differences are not so much in species as in habit. Water-loving things, be they microbes, mushrooms, or Douglas firs, are literally in their element. Their growth and functioning in the life community are stepped up here.

With all its exuberance, the whole forest is unexpectedly fragile. The trees are shallow-rooted, as they can be where food and water are plentiful and where the forest cover is so continuous that the wind cannot easily get a "bite."

Within the rain forest, trees grow large and undergrowth is abundant. Olympic has the world's record specimens of Douglas fir, Western red cedar, and Western hemlock. The undergrowth, though luxuriant, is seldom impenetrable. In places it is yielding and pleasant to the touch, with winding aisles that invite strolling. The foliage is kept in check partly by the browsing of the park's most famous wild creature, the Roosevelt elk, who spend 9 months of the year here before migrating to high ground for the summer.

CAUSES OF WASHINGTON RAIN FOREST

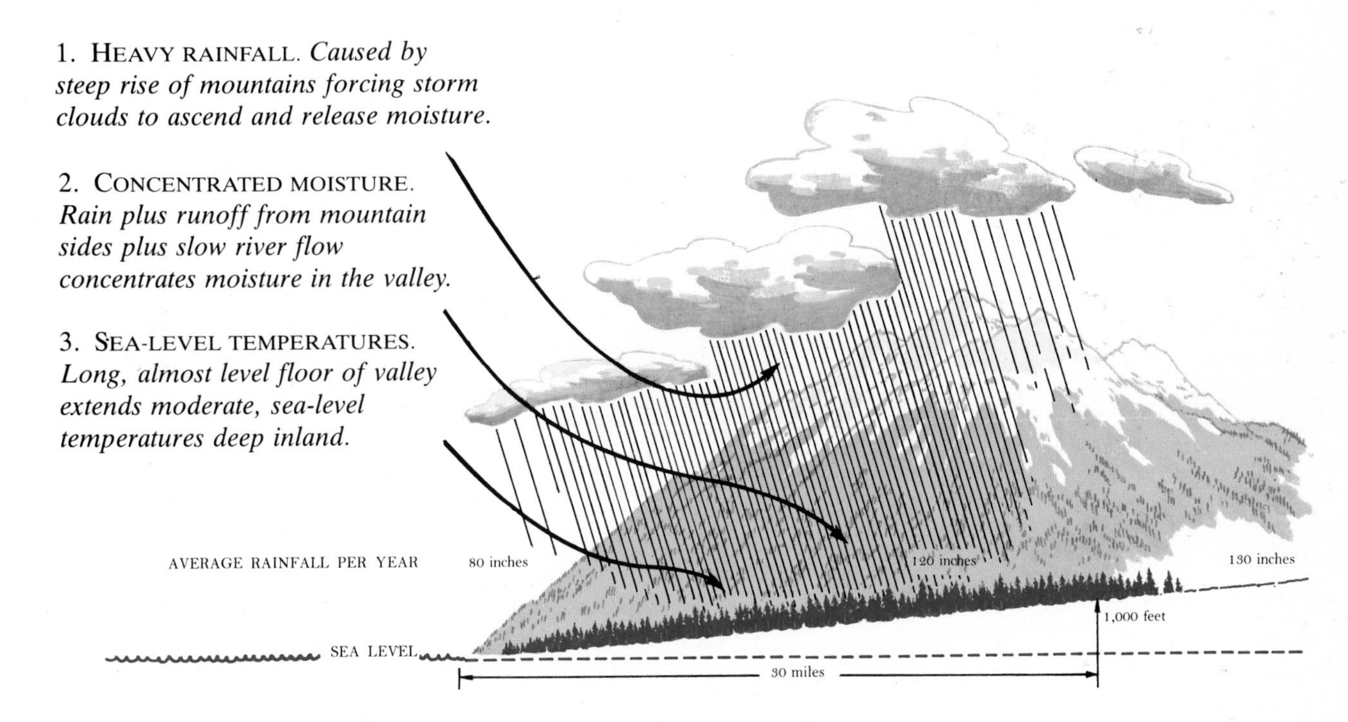

SOFT SUNLIGHT *filters through the green of the Olympic rain forest, inviting the visitor to stroll beneath moss-festooned trees through luxuriant growths of ferns, oxalis, bedstraw, and other plants in the diverse forest understory.*

DAVID MUENCH

Pacific Coast Area

With the hard, wet sand underfoot, the beach hiker finds the Pacific Coast Area a fascinating realm of spray and mist, where every twisting mile reveals subtle changes in the scenery and surprises along the trail.

The wide trail picks its way through barricades of driftwood, tossed on the beach by the waves in massive piles of jackstraws. Wedged among the rocks or bobbing in the surf are occasional glass floats, broken loose from fishing nets off Japan and carried across the Pacific by the current on a year-long voyage. Here and there are battered timbers and twisted ironwork, mementos of the countless ships that have been smashed to bits against the cliffs.

In season, the running of the smelt brings out fishermen en masse; and during the clamming months, throngs of diggers, equipped with shovels and buckets, probe feverishly for razor clams that retreat deep into the sand to elude the clutching hand. An abundance of marine life thrives in the tide pools, where it may be viewed under the guidance of ranger naturalists, who conduct walks through this chill and slippery realm.

BETTY RANDALL

Tide pools rich with sea life *will most likely reward the persevering viewer—perhaps by the sight of a starfish, spiny sea urchin, flowerlike sea anemone, or scurrying hermit crab.*

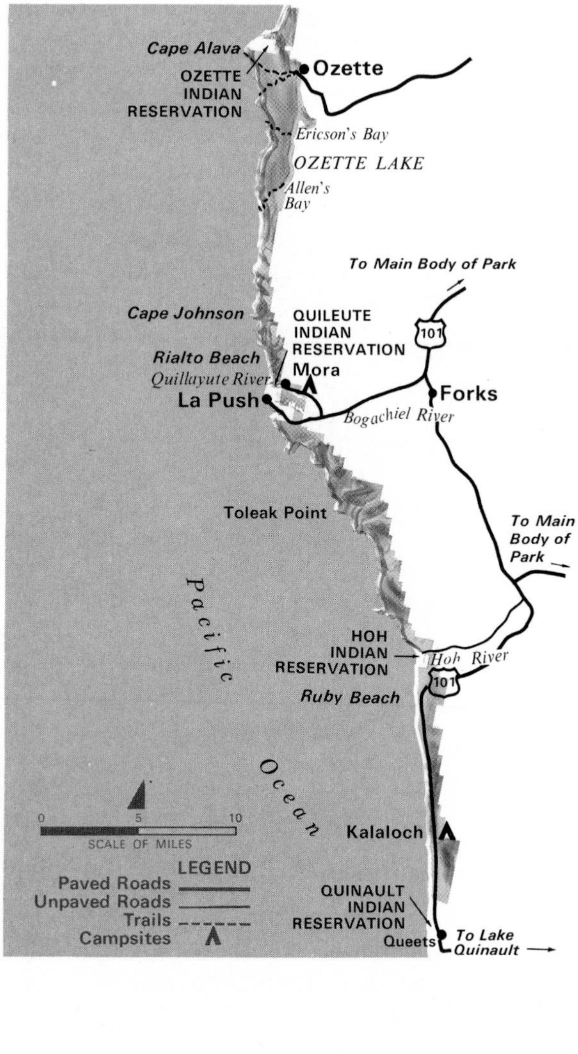

Cape Alava
OZETTE INDIAN RESERVATION
Ozette
Ericson's Bay
OZETTE LAKE
Allen's Bay
To Main Body of Park
Cape Johnson
QUILEUTE INDIAN RESERVATION
101
Rialto Beach
Quillayute River
Mora
La Push
Forks
Bogachiel River
Toleak Point
To Main Body of Park
Pacific Ocean
HOH INDIAN RESERVATION
Hoh River
101
Ruby Beach
0 5 10
SCALE OF MILES
Kalaloch
LEGEND
Paved Roads
Unpaved Roads
Trails
Campsites
QUINAULT INDIAN RESERVATION
Queets
To Lake Quinault

Coastal strip *of Olympic National Park is separated from the main body of the park that lies a few miles inland.*

ED COOPER

GIANT SEA STACKS *reflect in glistening, wave-smoothed sand at the ocean's edge. Tough remnants of original strata that once extended much farther seaward, these rocks and islets offer refuge for 75 species of coastal birds.*

"HOLE-IN-THE-WALL" *at Rialto Beach provides striking subject matter for photographers as well as passage through the rocky headland. The only way to really see this incomparable coastline is by walking. Hikers travel the beach between sea and forest, climbing over steep headlands or skirting them at low tide.* DAVID MUENCH

POLISHED SMOOTH BY THE ELEMENTS, *a giant driftwood sculpture frames a view of beachcombers. Winter storms pound this coast with waves that toss enormous logs ashore as if they were matchsticks, but cloudy skies and damp weather don't deter those who are drawn to this dramatic, unspoiled coastline.*

DAVID MUENCH

Hikers' Highlands

THE HEART OF THE PARK IS A DEDICATED MOUNTAIN WILDERNESS. Without question, it is not for everyone. Yet, even with all the aloofness of haughty Olympus itself, no other wilderness is more inviting, more unlocked, or more approachable.

This highland domain is all up-and-down country, its peaks and ridges separated by the valleys of rivers sliced so deep into the yielding rock that some have reached their ultimate level. Irregular and complex as they are, the Olympics contain two principal sections: a "wet" area that roughly faces the western boundary of the park and traps the bulk of the moisture-laden air from the Pacific Ocean, and a "dry" section that marks the eastern edge with a series of peaks separated by short, steep, river canyons. Mount Olympus, monarch of the wet range, is not easy to see from afar. Unlike its distant neighbor, Mount Rainier, which rises high above the countryside, Olympus is a puzzling cluster of crags that are barely clear of the ice cap and nearly lost in a jumble of peaks.

Few roads penetrate to this mountain fastness, and access is largely by trail—600 miles of it. Hikers familiar with conditions in the Sierra or Rockies find the Olympics easy going because of the lower altitudes, the fresh, cool weather, plentiful water, and soft, spongy trails.

G. C. KELLEY

AN ADEPT PEOPLE-WATCHER, *a curious marmot peers from his rocky hideaway near Hurricane Ridge. Watchdogs of the high trails, marmots are often seen above timberline. Their shrill whistles inform their relatives up the trail that non-marmots are approaching. These self-important little animals are cousins of the prairie dog, but are found only at higher elevations.*

THIS IS A HIKER'S PARK. *Breathtaking vistas open with every bend in the trail. The up-and-down terrain produces long views of deep canyons, towering mountain ridges, and meadows that are incredibly filled with wildflowers in early summer.*

BETTY RANDALL

A SILENT, WHITE WORLD *surrounds this hiker on Mount Angeles. In the distance, moisture-laden clouds linger over Mount Olympus. This is a good day hike from the Hurricane Ridge Road. For those who want company on their snowshoe walks or cross-country ski tours, park naturalists conduct a full schedule of winter activities.*

KEITH GUNNAR

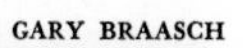

GARY BRAASCH

BETTY RANDALL

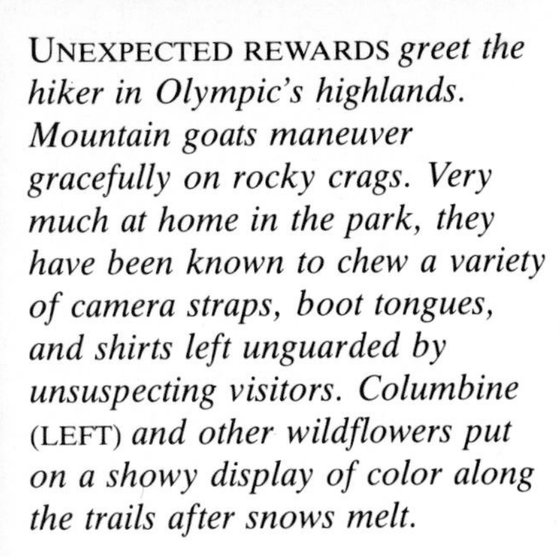

UNEXPECTED REWARDS *greet the hiker in Olympic's highlands. Mountain goats maneuver gracefully on rocky crags. Very much at home in the park, they have been known to chew a variety of camera straps, boot tongues, and shirts left unguarded by unsuspecting visitors. Columbine* (LEFT) *and other wildflowers put on a showy display of color along the trails after snows melt.*

MOUNT RAINIER

SNOW-CAPPED BEACON TO A STATE

PARK FACTS: *Location:* West central Washington. *Discovered:* 1792. *Established:* March 2, 1899. *Size:* 378 sq. mi. *Altitude:* 1,914 to 14,410 ft. *Climate:* Mt. Rainier perennially snow and cloud capped. *Season:* All year. *Annual visitors:* 2,095,000. *Accommodations:* Lodges (May-October), campgrounds. *Activities:* Rock and ice climbing (mountaineering school), hiking, cross-country skiing, snow sliding. *Information:* Supt., Mt. Rainier National Park, Ashford, WA 98304.

ON A CLEAR DAY, THE SNOW-MANTLED CREST OF MOUNT RAINIER dominates the skyline of northwest Washington, even in cities and towns on Puget Sound more than 50 miles away. At a distance its great height and some trick of the atmosphere make it seem much closer. Those who live within sight of its gleaming peak seem to draw a sense of security and well-being from its presence; they are cheered when the clouds roll away and they can tell one another, "You can see the mountain today."

It is easy to imagine the impact the mountain had on Captain George Vancouver of the British Navy, when he cruised the Pacific Coast in 1792. He was probably the first white man to see it, and he promptly gave it its present name, in honor of his friend Admiral Peter Rainier. Later it became an unmistakable landmark for pioneers bound for the Oregon Country, who knew when they saw it that they were nearing the end of their journey.

The mountain was born of fire. It is one of several great volcanoes of the Cascade Range, and it inspired John Muir to write: "Of all the fire mountains which, like beacons, once blazed along the Pacific Coast, Mount Rainier is the noblest."

Despite the steam caves and warm mineral springs that prove the volcanic furnaces are not completely extinguished, more than one-tenth of Mount Rainier National Park's 378-square-mile area is ice. There are a dozen major glaciers, and 26 that are important enough to have names; and they are among the most accessible in the United States. Some can be reached by a short walk from the road, and several others can be viewed from close-up vantage points. Until recently, for as long as men have been studying them, the glaciers have

A MOUNTAIN BEYOND IMAGINING, *Rainier towers two miles above the surrounding foothills. In a land rich with peaks, this one is known simply as "the mountain." Here it reveals its west side to hikers at Klapatche Park.*

DAVID MUENCH

A MIRROR IMAGE *of Rainier shimmers on Reflection Lake. Good roads in the park, and the 90-mile Wonderland Trail that encircles the mountain, provide short walking approaches to grand views of the mountain from all sides. There's hardly a corner of the park you can't visit on a day's walk.*

ED COOPER

MOUNT RAINIER NATIONAL PARK

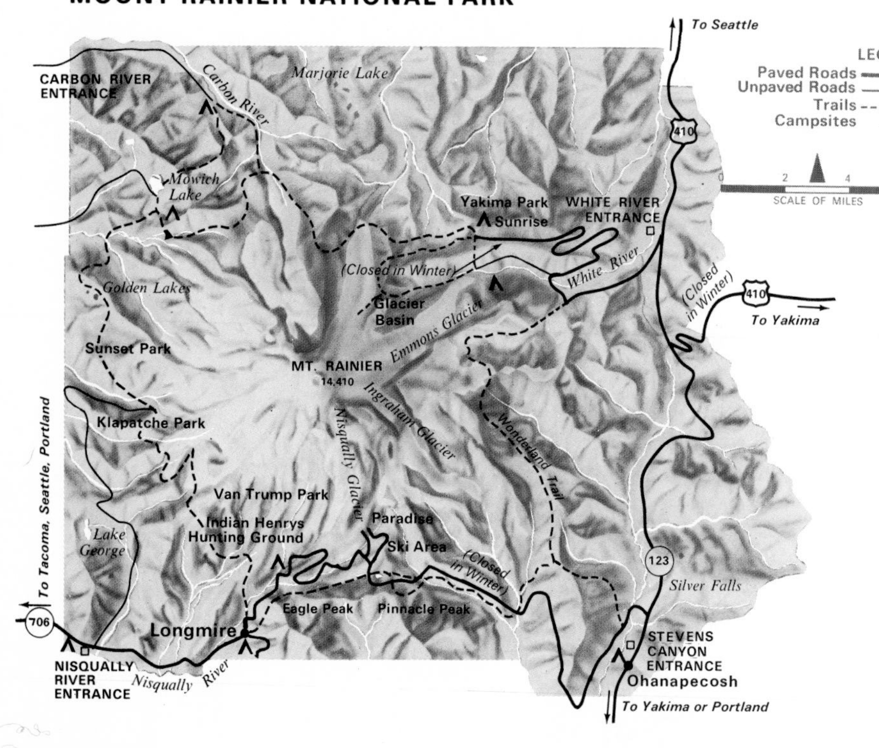

MASSIVE MOUNT RAINIER *sprawls over roughly half of the park's 378 square miles. Twenty-six glaciers, covering 40 square miles, grind down the slopes of the enormous extinct volcano.*

been gradually receding. Now some are advancing again—very slowly, of course, and perhaps only temporarily.

Below the ice fields is an unspoiled preserve of alpine meadows and dense forests, home of countless birds and animals—tiny as the chickadee, large as the black bear, rare as the mountain goat. Wildflowers brighten the lower slopes in late spring and move upward in an unfolding tapestry as the snow melts.

Rainier rations its beauty and grandeur, as if to make sure it will be appreciated. Much of the time it retires behind a heavy cloud cover; on other days it tantalizes its admirers by hiding behind a thin curtain of vapor. Then, when the mood is right, the veil suddenly is lifted, and there is the matchless crown of ice and snow shining in the sunlight.

Weather is uncertain at Mount Rainier, but a good share of warm, clear days can usually be expected between early July and mid-September, and sometimes into October, when the wooded slopes renew their annual display of autumn color. In the course of the year the park receives heavy rain and snowfall, for the Cascades are a major barrier to moisture-laden winds from the Pacific. Precipitation averages about 110 inches a year at Paradise, where as much as 90 feet of snow has fallen in a single winter to leave a snowpack of 30 feet.

Hiking is popular here, and the choice of trails ranges from short nature walks to a hike along the Wonderland Trail, which completely encircles the mountain and samples the whole variety of terrain the park has to offer. Typical of the shorter walks is the Trail of the Shadows, a special delight in spring when the rivulets are full and the air is fragrant with the odor of evergreens, damp earth, and growing things.

For those who enjoy mountain climbing, Rainier is a worthy challenge. It requires a strenuous ascent over lava, glaciers, and ice fields, though without the danger of the vertical faces to be scaled elsewhere in the West. Some 3,000 independent climbers—after registering in person with a ranger and obtaining weather forecasts, route condition information, and other helpful recommendations—and an additional 1,000 guided climbers reach the summit each year.

The park is open year round, although the Carbon River, White River, and Stevens Canyon entrances are closed from the first heavy snowfall (usually around November 1) until about the last half of June. Mount Rainier is a favorite of campers, and one of the campgrounds—Sunshine Point, near Nisqually Entrance—is available for use through the winter. On winter weekends and holidays, cross-country skiers come to the park.

In several ways Mount Rainier is one of the least remote of the national parks of the West. Its peak is visible over a vast area. It is one of the nearest to large centers of population. And, in a sense, it can be seen from the highway by the passerby, for the roads along the southern and eastern edges provide spectacular views of its snow-clad monarch.

But few who glimpse its beauty as they pass are satisfied until they return for a longer visit.

HOW DOES A GLACIER WORK?

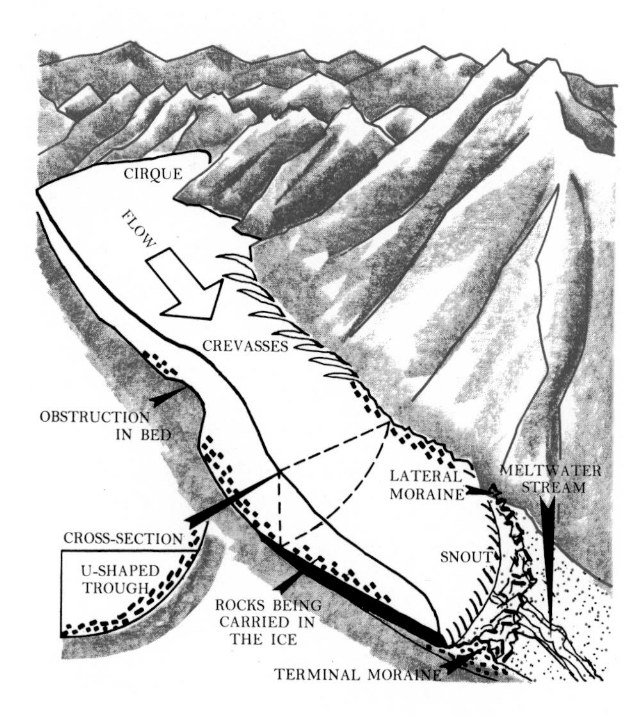

GLACIERS ARE FORMED *where snowfall is so heavy that the winter's accumulation cannot be carried off by evaporation in spring. The snow piles deeper and deeper, becomes denser and denser, and finally turns to a near-solid—ice. The tremendous weight of the built-up mass causes it to slide downhill at a slow pace. Where the river of ice reaches lower and warmer elevations, it melts and changes to a running stream or river. At the point where its progress is arrested, it forms a bulging tongue called a "snout."*

The flowing ice carries rock debris with it, some dislodged from the mountainsides, some from the bed of the valley that it occupies. This residue gives the lower end of a glacier a dirty, messy look quite unlike the pristine white of its upper reaches. In time, the rocky mass is deposited either at the sides or at the snout in massive accumulations known as moraines. The gouging processes of a glacier are most active where it starts, thus causing the formation of bowl-like cavities known as cirques.

KEITH GUNNAR

TOP-OF-THE-WORLD ADVENTURE *draws mountaineers from near and far to Rainier's flanks. The sleeping volcano presents nearly every imaginable climbing challenge, and has been a training ground for expeditions headed for peaks from Alaska to the Himalayas. Ice and rock-climbing courses are given on the mountain, but Rainier also offers gentler routes that anyone in good health and with determination can climb under the supervision of the park-sanctioned guide service.* ABOVE: *A climber descends Ingraham Glacier, one of six glaciers that originate at the summit.*

HARALD SUND

SO BIG IT MAKES ITS OWN WEATHER, *the mountain is breathtaking when viewed close up after a fresh, powdery snowfall. On clear winter days, it is a stunning, mirage-like sight that can be seen from almost every city in Washington.*

BOB AND IRA SPRING

"A PERFECT FLOWER ELYSIUM," *is the way John Muir described the wildflower parks that encircle Mount Rainier. A bright wreath of ever-changing color carpets slopes between glaciers and forest. Floral display comes in two intense bloom periods: first in early July, as snow recedes; second in August.*

PAUL V. THOMAS

Canadian dogwood

Phlox

Buttercup

Avalanche lily

ED COOPER

SPRING SNOW MELT *brings streams rushing down Rainier's flanks. Clear and swift Edith Creek tumbles through a boulder-strewn corridor on its way to join the Paradise River just a short distance away.*

HIGHEST FALLS IN THE PARK, *320-foot Comet Falls are reached by a 2½-mile trail that climbs 1,900 feet from Christine Falls parking lot. Glimpses of mountain goats, views of glaciers, and flower-blanketed meadows reward your efforts.*

ED COOPER

CRATER LAKE

BLUE SAUCER ON A VOLCANO SITE

PARK FACTS: *Location:* Southwestern Oregon. *Discovered:* June 12, 1853. *Established:* May 22, 1902. *Size:* 250 sq. mi. *Altitude:* 4,405 to 8,926 ft. *Climate:* Snow covers park nearly 8 months of year; South and West entrance roads kept open all year. Summer weather very unpredictable, with warm days and chilly nights. *Annual visitors:* 580,000. *Accommodations:* Lodge and cabins (mid-June to mid-September), campgrounds (mid-June to September 30). *Activities:* Boat tours, bus tours, cross-country skiing. *Information:* Supt., Crater Lake, OR 97604.

THE KLAMATH INDIANS TELL US that long ago, before there was a Crater Lake, the volcanic mountain called Mazama served as the passageway between the domain below the earth and the world topside. When Llao, chief of the world below, visited the surface, he could be seen as a dark form towering above the white snows. When Scell, chief of the world above, appeared on earth, he rested atop Mount Shasta, south of Mazama.

The day came when these two deities quarreled, and the anger of Llao shook the ground, sent thunder and burning ashes into the sky, and spilled lava down the mountainside.

The medicine men interpreted Llao's violence as a curse directed at least in part toward the tribe for wickedness and error. To make atonement, they climbed to the top of Mount Mazama and threw themselves into the crater.

The chief of the world above was so impressed by this sacrifice that he renewed his war with Llao and finally drove him underground. As the chief of the world below retreated and disappeared, the mountaintop fell in upon him and his door to the surface was sealed. Never again did Llao frighten the Indians; the crater of his mountain filled with pure waters and became a scene of peace and quiet.

The Indian legends have helped geologists reconstruct the violent eruptions that climaxed with the collapse of Mount Mazama's cone. The timetable is necessarily inexact, but all evidence indicates that the bowl containing Crater Lake was created within about the last 6,600 years.

Before its collapse, Mazama was a 12,000-foot volcano that stood out with the mountains now called Baker, Rainier, Adams, Hood, and Shasta as giants of the Cascade Range. The peak had built up from repeated flows of molten lava

INTENSE BLUE *of Crater Lake must be seen to be believed. A sparkling jewel cradled by encircling cliffs, it is the deepest lake (1,932 feet) in the United States. Only six lakes in the world are deeper. Its color ranges from indigo to turquoise depending on the light, weather, and season.*

DAVID MUENCH

and the debris of explosive eruptions. Glaciers filled the valleys of its sculptured slopes, and thick forests covered the foothills.

The climactic eruptions recounted in legend must have been horrendous by any standards. Earthquakes were followed by enormous clouds of gases and steam that blocked out the sun for weeks. Embers and ashes fell over a vast area, covering the land with gray powder and igniting the forests. The glaciers melted and new rivers washed down the steep slopes.

And then came the greatest explosion of all. A dense cloud of dust, expanding gases, and red-hot lava fragments burst from the crater and spilled down the slopes, traveling at great speed. The avalanche crushed every form of life for 35 miles around.

Long fissures opened beneath the volcano. The violence underground continued for days, with additional eruptions and expulsions, until Mazama's peak became a heavy shell over an empty pocket. Shaken by the violence and deprived of support, the top of the volcano fell in with a roar that must literally have staggered the Indian witnesses.

When the skies finally cleared, the mountain peak was gone, and the foreshortened slopes of Mazama rose to a huge bowl more than 5 miles across and 4,000 feet deep.

The caldera (Spanish and Portuguese for caldron) began to fill with rain and melting snow. The first pools were turned to steam by the boiling mud and hot rocks in the bottom of the basin, but as the mountain cooled, the caldera filled with water. Eventually the water level reached a point higher than that of today, then receded to its present surface elevation of 6,176 feet.

There are many calderas in the world, but none is quite as spectacular as that of Crater Lake. The broken lines of the old volcano contrast with the quiet surface of the deep, blue water. Visitors who drive around the lake are impressed with the immensity of the mountain and the tremendous forces that caused its downfall. Geologists find Mazama one of the best places on earth to study volcanism.

Most of the park's roadways and points of interest are related to the caldera and its surrounding slopes. The major exception is the Pinnacles. These needle-like rock formations are remnants of the avalanches of volcanic pumice that preceded Mount Mazama's collapse. The pumice spread out in sheets and cooled rapidly on top, but the hot rocks beneath continued to send gases to the surface through vents. These hot emissions hardened the pumice around the vents to form "pipes." When the rest of the pumice eroded away during succeeding centuries, the pipes remained as thin pinnacles.

The Indians long believed that only punishment could come to men who looked upon a lake that was sacred to the spirits. "Do not look upon this place," the legend warned, "for it will mean death or lasting sorrow." Fortunately, the ominous warning no longer applies. The thousands who stand in awe each year on the brink of Crater Lake come away not in sorrow but with a new and exultant realization of nature's power and beauty.

HOW CRATER LAKE WAS FORMED

1. ERUPTIONS *of lava from crater built up Mt. Mazama over a period of time.*

2. THE VOLCANO *spent itself in a series of violent eruptions that emptied the underlying lava chamber.*

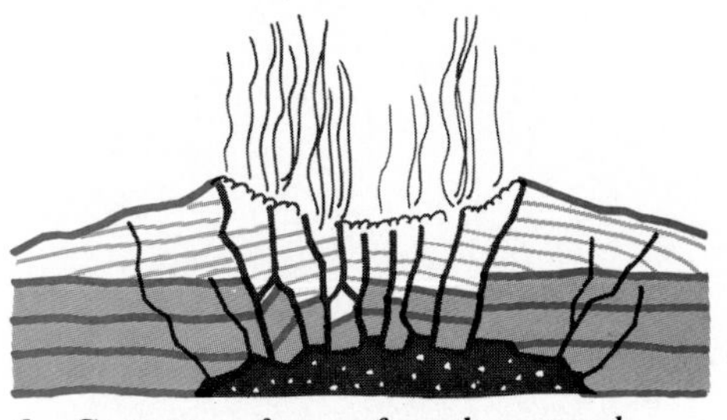

3. CAVE-IN *of top of peak, caused by the withdrawal of underground support, created a caldera.*

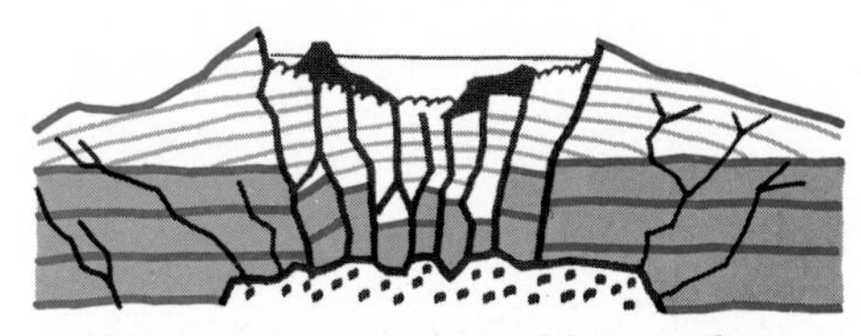

4. WATER FILLED *the caldera to form a lake. Wizard Island was formed 6,000 years later by a new eruption.*

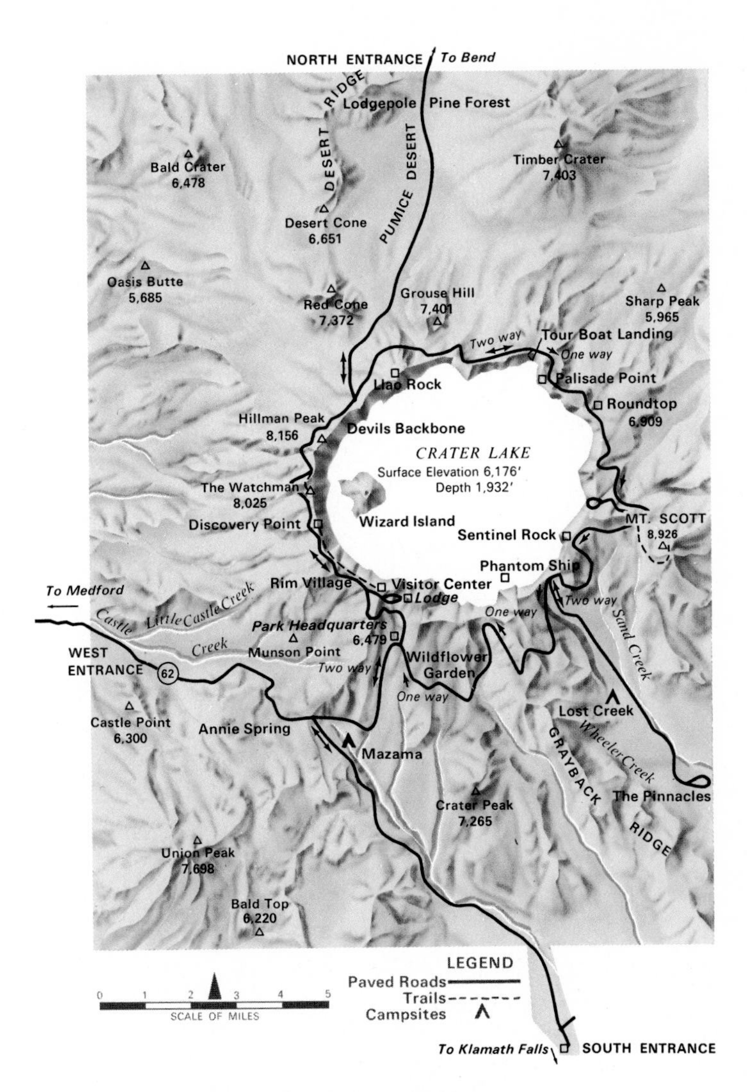

CRATER LAKE NATIONAL PARK

CORE OF THE *250-square-mile national park, Crater Lake's 22 square miles of water is contained within a 25-mile circle of cliffs. The pumice that spewed out of the crater of now-dead Mt. Mazama filled all the valleys now within the park boundaries and raced 20-30 miles to east and west. Lighter pumice, blasted into the air, was wind-borne for 80 miles and covered 5,000 square miles.*

ED COOPER

PHANTOM SHIP *seems to float across the still surface of the lake. Its brownish sails are part of a volcanic dike; the pale hull is formed of volcanic ash. For a closer look at the unique rock remnant, take the sightseeing boat in summer for a two-hour trip around the lake.*

GLOWING AVALANCHES *once filled the valleys surrounding ancient Mt. Mazama with a white-hot blanket of pumice. As the pumice cooled, hot steam and gases were released through vents, which cooked into hard-baked chimneys as at the Pinnacles* (LEFT). *The lava cone of Wizard Island* (BELOW) *rises near the lake shore. On a boat trip around the lake, you can stop over on the island and hike to the top of the cone.*

ED COOPER

ED COOPER

REDWOOD

SANCTUARY FOR THE WORLD'S TALLEST TREES

PARK FACTS: *Location:* North coast of California. *Discovered:* 1769. *Established:* October 2, 1968. *Size:* 166 sq. mi. (includes 3 state parks). *Altitude:* Sea level. *Climate:* Damp, cool summers. *Season:* All year. *Annual visitors:* 513,400. *Accommodations:* Campgrounds in state parks. *Activities:* Hiking, guided tide pool walks, kayak trips on Smith River. *Information:* Supt., Redwood National Park, Drawer N, Crescent City, CA 95531.

ALONG A STRIP OF THE NORTHERN CALIFORNIA shoreline grows one of the world's most unusual trees, the coast redwood, renowned almost equally for its majestic beauty and for its commercial value as a source of lumber with many unique properties.

The towering trees, some of them a thousand years old, soar into the sky to 300 feet or more, the tallest rising higher than the torch of the Statue of Liberty. The trees grow in dense groves in a fog belt along the coast, favoring river valleys or canyons that open to the sea. In their natural state, the redwoods shed their lower branches as they mature and form a canopy a hundred feet overhead, creating the illusion of a great natural cathedral, which visitors find both inspiring and humbling. Unfortunately for the fate of the stately trees, the demand for redwood lumber is so great—it resists shrinkage, rot, and decay—that only good timber management can forestall the eventual logging of all the redwood trees in California. As a safeguard against such a disaster, thousands of acres of virgin redwoods have been set aside for perpetuity under government protection. Of this sequestered land, 58,000 acres became part of the national park system in 1968. In 1978, the park was enlarged by a 48,000-acre addition at the southern end. Included in the national park are three state parks, totaling 27,000 acres. These state park units are administered by the California Department of Parks and Recreation. In time, they will probably be donated to the federal preserve and the whole complex administered as one, but for the time being, the two systems operate as cooperating but separate entities.

STATELY TREES *rise above a dense forest cover of ferns, rhododendrons, and other plants that thrive in the shade cast by the interweaving branches a hundred feet above them.*

DAVID MUENCH

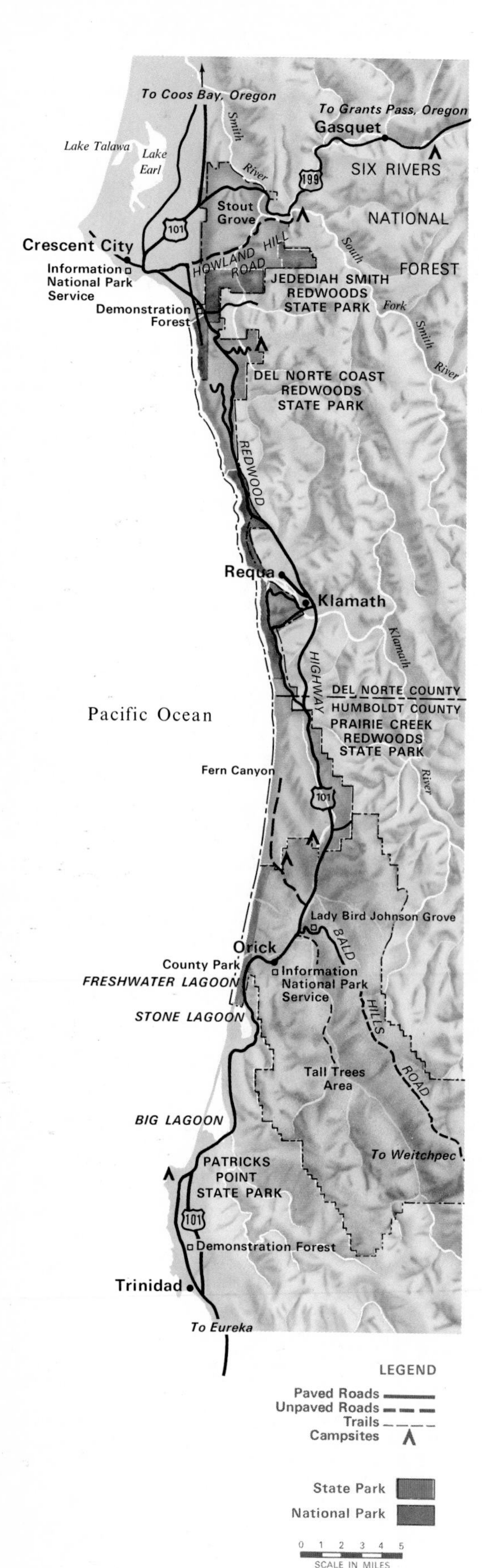

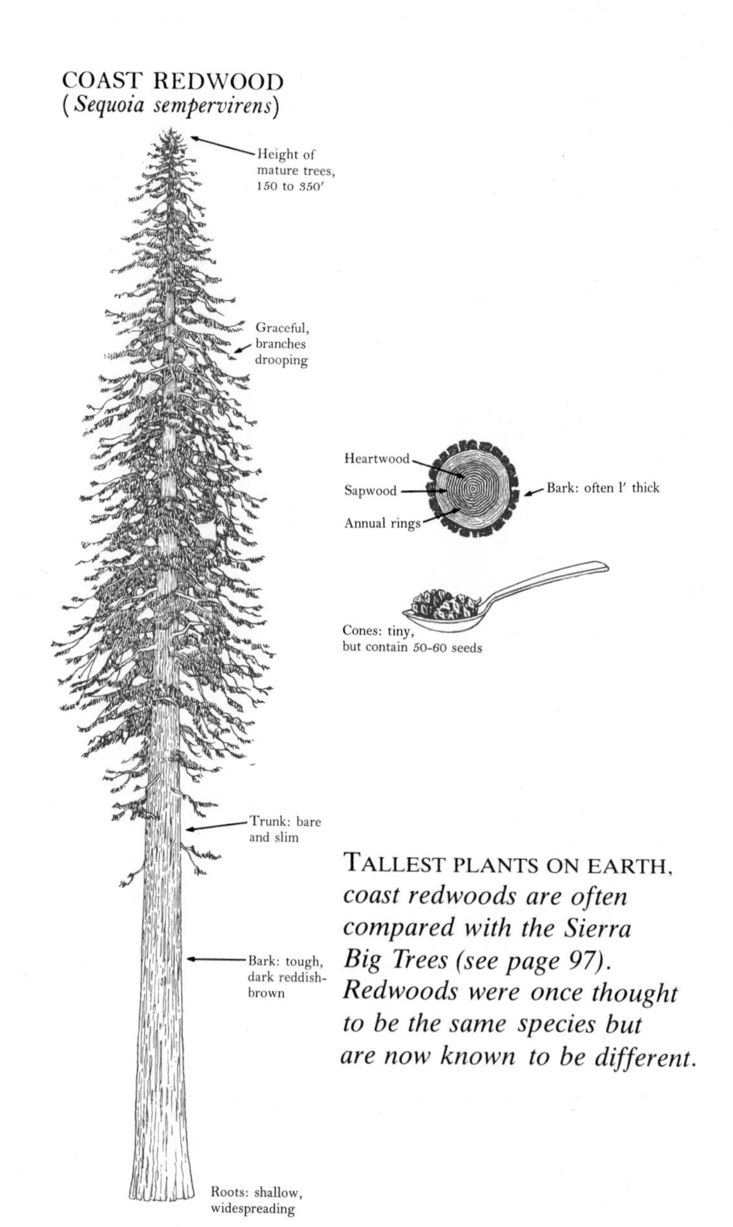

TALLEST PLANTS ON EARTH, *coast redwoods are often compared with the Sierra Big Trees (see page 97). Redwoods were once thought to be the same species but are now known to be different.*

REDWOOD NATIONAL PARK

THE COMBINATION *of national park and state park lands may be confusing to travelers who move from one jurisdiction to another in just a few miles—or even a few steps. However, in time the state parks inside the national park boundaries will probably be donated to the National Park System.*

AUTUMN IN THE REDWOODS *brings a special mood. Crowds leave, the summer fog gives way to sparkling days, and splashes of bright autumn color contrast with the somber redwoods that tower alongside the roads.*

JOSEF MUENCH

PHILIP HYDE

REDWOODS FAVOR THE FOG BELT *close to the ocean, where mists roll in during the summer and as much as 100 inches of rain may fall in winter. In some groves, rhododendron blossoms brighten the mist-shrouded forest. Along the shore, the waves wash some 50 miles of ocean front protected within the park's boundaries. At low tide, ranger naturalists conduct nature walks to tide pools. Collecting tide pool life is forbidden.*

PHILIP HYDE

LASSEN VOLCANIC

THE SMOKE CLOUD ROSE FIVE MILES

PARK FACTS: *Location:* North central California. *Discovered:* Probably in early 1800s. *Established:* August 9, 1916. *Size:* 160 sq. mi. *Altitude:* 4,822 to 10,457 ft. *Climate:* Warm, pleasant summers; snow in winter. *Season:* All year, but transpark road closed by snow. *Annual visitors:* 442,200. *Accommodations:* Guest ranch (July 1 to Labor Day), campgrounds (mid-May to October). *Activities:* Hiking, boating, horseback riding, skiing and snow recreation area in southern section of the park, cross-country skiing (Manzanita Lake). *Information:* Supt., Lassen Volcanic National Park, Mineral, CA 96063.

WHEN THE FIRST SETTLERS CAME to north central California, they assumed that volcanic Lassen Peak was extinct. The earth around it was pockmarked with bubbling sinks, but the mountain itself appeared cold and lifeless.

But on May 30, 1914, they changed their minds. Without warning, a great column of steam and gases spouted from the top of the peak, throwing out small pieces of lava and debris on the upper slopes. The eruption was brief, but it opened a new vent in the old crater and signaled the beginning of renewed activity that lasted more than seven years.

Lassen erupted more than 150 times during the next year, spouting dust and steam high in the air and flinging cinders and small boulders around its base. But no lava appeared, and spectators were more curious than concerned.

During the winter of 1914-15, snowfall was unusually heavy. It piled deep on the upper slopes of Lassen, and all that fell within the new crater immediately melted and drained down into the earth. Some scientists believe that this build-up of water below the surface was partly responsible for what happened in the spring.

On the evening of May 19, molten lava bubbled up to the crater rim. On the southwest edge, it trickled over and flowed a thousand feet down the side before cooling into a solid sheet. On the northeast side, a much more dramatic performance was developing. Lava spilled over the rim, steam roared out of a hole in the mountainside near the top, and chunks of lava fell on the slopes. The heat melted the deep drifts of snow, and this water combined with the debris of earlier eruptions to create a devastating mudflow. The deluge of mud surged down the mountain, growing in volume and violence, and funneled into the

QUIESCENT LASSEN PEAK *looms above the scene of its devastating eruptions of 1914-15. The mineral-rich soil and plentiful water have encouraged luxuriant growth of conifers and shrubby plants.*

PHILIP HYDE

valleys of Hat and Lost creeks. It peeled the bark off trees up to 18 feet and submerged the meadows with as much as 6 feet of debris.

Despite this cataclysm, Lassen Peak was not yet spent. Three days later a spectacular column of smoke mounted 5 miles into the air and a blast of steam shot out of the mountainside. This time the force of the steam jet was horizontal. Trees in its path were knocked down like matchsticks, and the earth was scrubbed bare.

With that release of pressure, Lassen seemed all but appeased. The volcano shuddered a few more times but by 1921 all visible activity had subsided.

There are still many signs of these volcanic eruptions—which are the most recent in the United States except for Hawaii and Alaska—but nature is gradually covering the wounds. The devastated area is clearly defined, although a few trees are taking root in the rocky debris. You can hike to the top of Lassen Peak and look into the crater, but the crucible has long since cooled and the mountain once again wears a cap of winter snow.

Well below the surface, however, the volcanic pot is still boiling. At those places where the crust is broken or cracked (there are six within the park), gases and steam hiss up through fumaroles and keep the mud bubbling like porridge on a hot stove. Sulfurous vapors taint the air.

Although the 1915 eruption poured forth molten lava, Lassen is actually a plug volcano, made of stiff lumps of lava pushed upward by subterranean forces but too thick to flow like liquid. Not old, it was probably formed no more than a few thousand years ago.

There are other significant examples of volcanism in Lassen Volcanic National Park. South of Lassen Peak are traces of another giant that once existed here—Mount Tehama, a huge cone 15 miles in diameter and 11,000 feet high. It eventually collapsed, and the fractured remnants include Brokeoff Mountain, Mount Diller, Pilot Pinnacle, Mount Conard, and Diamond Point.

Chaos Crags are the remains of four plug volcanoes, much like Lassen but without craters. Prospect Peak, Mount Harkness, Sifford Mountain, and Raker Peak are shield volcanoes similar to those of Hawaii—volcanoes that have been built up from layers of molten lava that flowed out and then cooled into "shields."

What about the future of Lassen Peak? Will it awaken again, or has it settled into a deep and lasting sleep? Many geologists believe the volcano is well on its way to extinction. The thermal activity underground continues, but only a few wisps of steam are ever seen atop the mountain. Another series of eruptions would come as a great surprise.

Of course, that's what they were saying back in 1913.

EVIDENCE OF VOLCANIC *activity dots the park landscape with cones, craters, fumaroles, vents.*

NATIONAL PARK SERVICE

FROM REFLECTION LAKE, *the 1915 eruption, only four airline miles away, was a spectacular sight. Over the centuries, stiff, pasty lava, too cool and viscous to flow downhill, squeezed up like toothpaste from a tube to form a dome-shaped peak rising 2,500 feet above its base.*

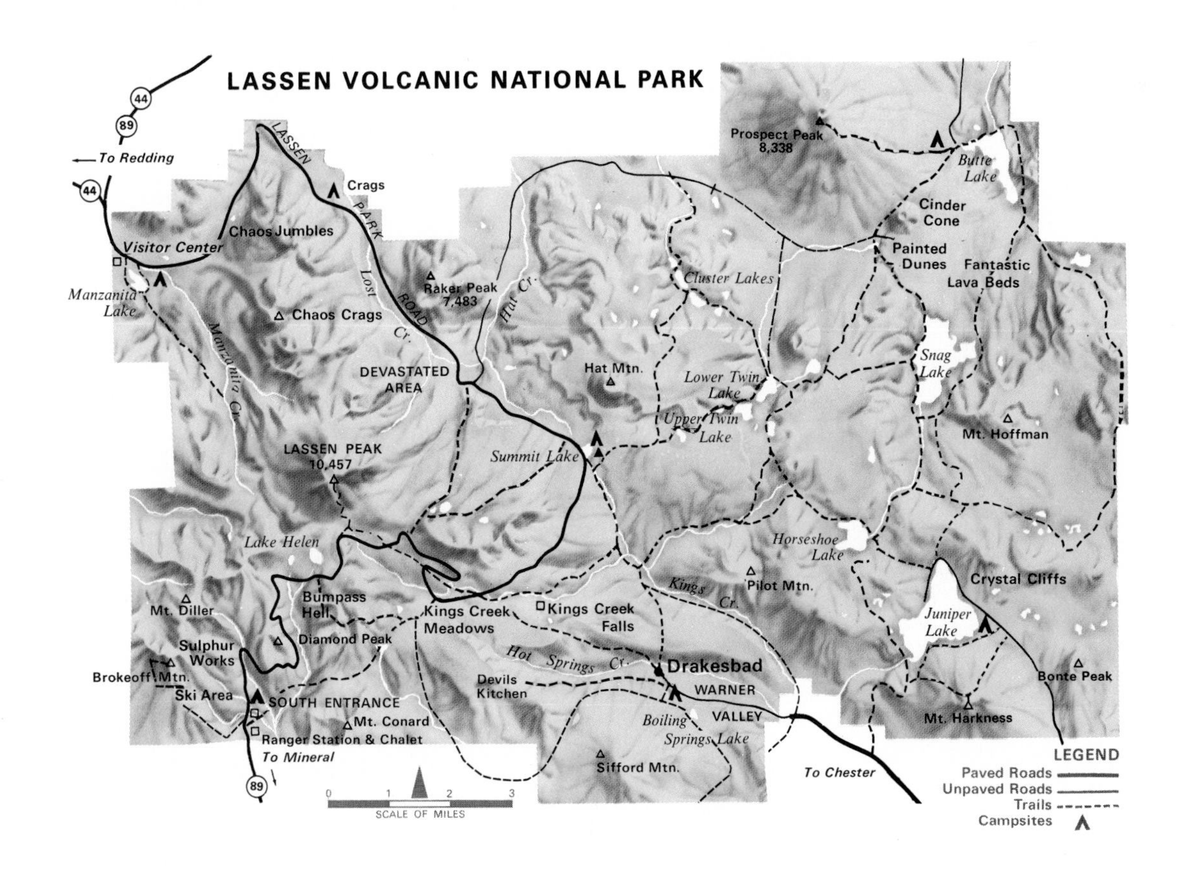

NATIONAL PARK SERVICE

TOURING PARTY *in 1915 watched the pyrotechnic display from a discreet distance. The smoke rose 5 miles into the sky and was visible for 50 miles. Five-ton rocks were hurled into the air.*

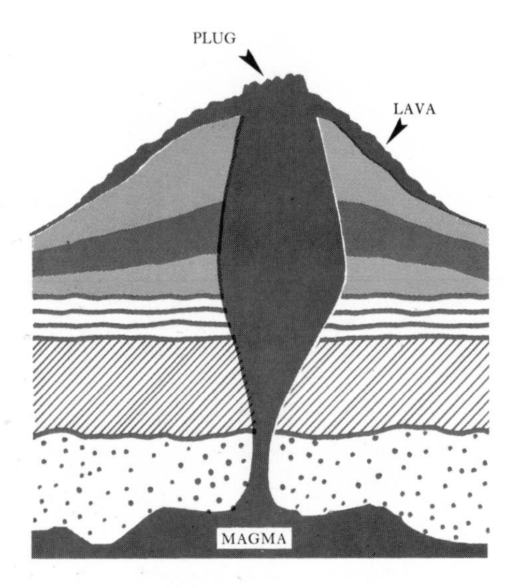

A VOLCANO BLOWS ITS TOP

A PLUG-DOME VOLCANO, *Lassen Peak began as stiff, pasty lava forced up like toothpaste from a tube.*

RAY ATKESON

FALL COMES EARLY *to Manzanita Lake and touches the alders and cottonwoods with orange and gold. Thus ends the short but luxuriant show of summer wildflowers. Soon winter sports enthusiasts will head for the slopes near the southwest entrance, and cross-country skiers will push deeper into the park.*

WILLIAM A. PAWEK

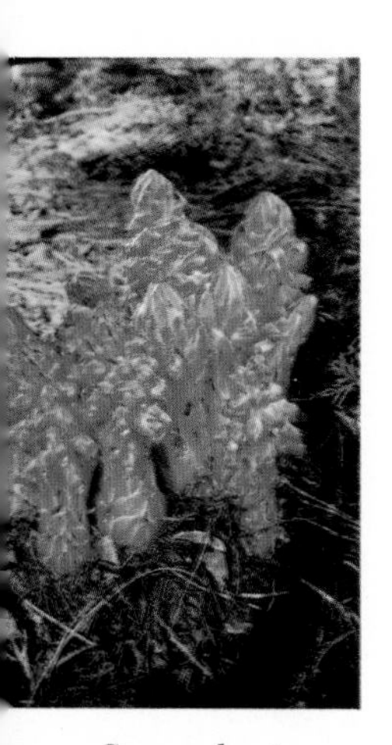

Snowplant

Penstemon

Indian paintbrush

Leopard lily

Lupine

RICHARD ROWAN

REEKING GASES *bubble up through hot mud at Sulphur Works* (LEFT) *near the southwest entrance. At Bumpass Hell* (BELOW), *rising steam and hissing vents give evidence of the thermal tumult close to the surface here.*

ED COOPER

PHILIP HYDE

FROM THE TOP OF CINDER CONE, *the peak of Mount Lassen is a snowy contrast on the horizon. Cinder Cone rises symmetrically 700 feet above the surrounding countryside. A true volcano (it erupted in 1851), it was formed of lava thrown out with explosive violence. When it reached the air, the lava cooled and dropped in an even fall of cinders.*

YOSEMITE

ICE, THE GREAT SCULPTOR

PARK FACTS: *Location:* East central California. *Discovered:* 1833. *Established:* State park, 1864; national park, 1890. *Size:* 1,189 sq. mi. *Altitude:* 2,000 to 13,114 ft. *Climate:* Dry, mild summers; relatively warm winters with heavy snow pack. *Season:* Valley, all year; high country, summer only. *Annual visitors:* 2,669,000. *Accommodations:* Hotels, lodges, cabins, tents, campgrounds. *Activities:* Hiking, horseback riding, biking (rentals), golfing, rock and ice climbing schools, tram tours, skiing (Badger Pass), cross-country skiing. *Information:* Supt., Yosemite National Park, CA 95389.

"AS I LOOKED AT THE GRANDEUR OF THE SCENE a peculiar exalted sensation seemed to fill my whole being, and I found my eyes in tears with emotion." So wrote one of the discoverers of Yosemite Valley in 1851, recording an experience that has moved thousands of visitors who have since followed the trail into the incomparable Valley.

Although it represents less than one-half of one percent of the total area of the park, the Valley contains more than its share of scenic beauty, and, historically, it accounts for the very existence of Yosemite as a national park.

The Valley was known to the Indians for centuries, but because of its remoteness and inaccessibility it was not discovered by white men until the 1850s, when the Gold Rush attracted thousands of inquisitive miners to the nearby foothills and made its disclosure inevitable. Though seen from the rim in 1833, it was a pair of miners, tracking a wounded bear in 1849, who were the first Americans to actually enter the Valley. They were followed two years later by a punitive expedition, known as the Mariposa Battalion, that entered the Valley in pursuit of Indians. Convinced that they had made an important discovery, they named the Valley, calling it "Yosemite," from the Ahwahneechee Indian word "Yo-shay-ma-tee." The translation was "some of them are killers," and referred to the grizzly bear.

Word of the discovery was slow in spreading, but by 1855 the first tourist parties had followed Indian trails into the Valley to look at the reported wonders. One enterprising young miner by the name of James Hutchings was so impressed by what he saw that he launched into the business of attracting and serving tourists. He started a journal, *Hutchings California Illustrated*, that featured Yosemite, published a series of guidebooks to the area, and built a hotel in the

MOST FAMOUS LANDMARK *in the park is Half Dome. The first white man to see the great monolith named it "Rock of Ages," but the name did not stick. It dominates the upper end of the Valley, rising 4,800 feet above the Valley floor.*

ED COOPER

Valley. Soon afterward, other hotels were opened, toll routes built, and the Valley began to welcome tourists of a sufficiently durable cast to survive the long and arduous trip by stage and saddle horse.

While commercial development was in progress, agitation for protection of the natural beauty of the park was also under way. John Muir and others published articles extolling the glories of the Valley, congressional interest in the area was aroused, and in 1864 President Lincoln issued the historic proclamation that ceded the Valley and the Mariposa Grove of Big Trees to California, "to be held for public use, resort, and recreation, unalienable for all time."

The Valley and the Mariposa Grove, 35 miles apart, were administered as a state park for 42 years before being returned to the federal government in 1906. In the meantime, a national park was established in 1890 that surrounded the original grant, and Yosemite was thus administered as two separate parks for 16 years. Administration of the national park was largely entrusted to units of the United States Cavalry until 1916.

Within the 1,189 square miles of the park today, there is of course a great deal more to see than the wonders compressed within the Valley. Glaciers, giant sequoias, alpine meadows, 13,000-foot Sierra peaks, emerald lakes, and sparkling streams are scattered in profusion throughout the vast domain. Those who know the park well know it as a rich and varied playground that is capable of sustaining years of rewarding exploration.

NATIONAL PARK SERVICE

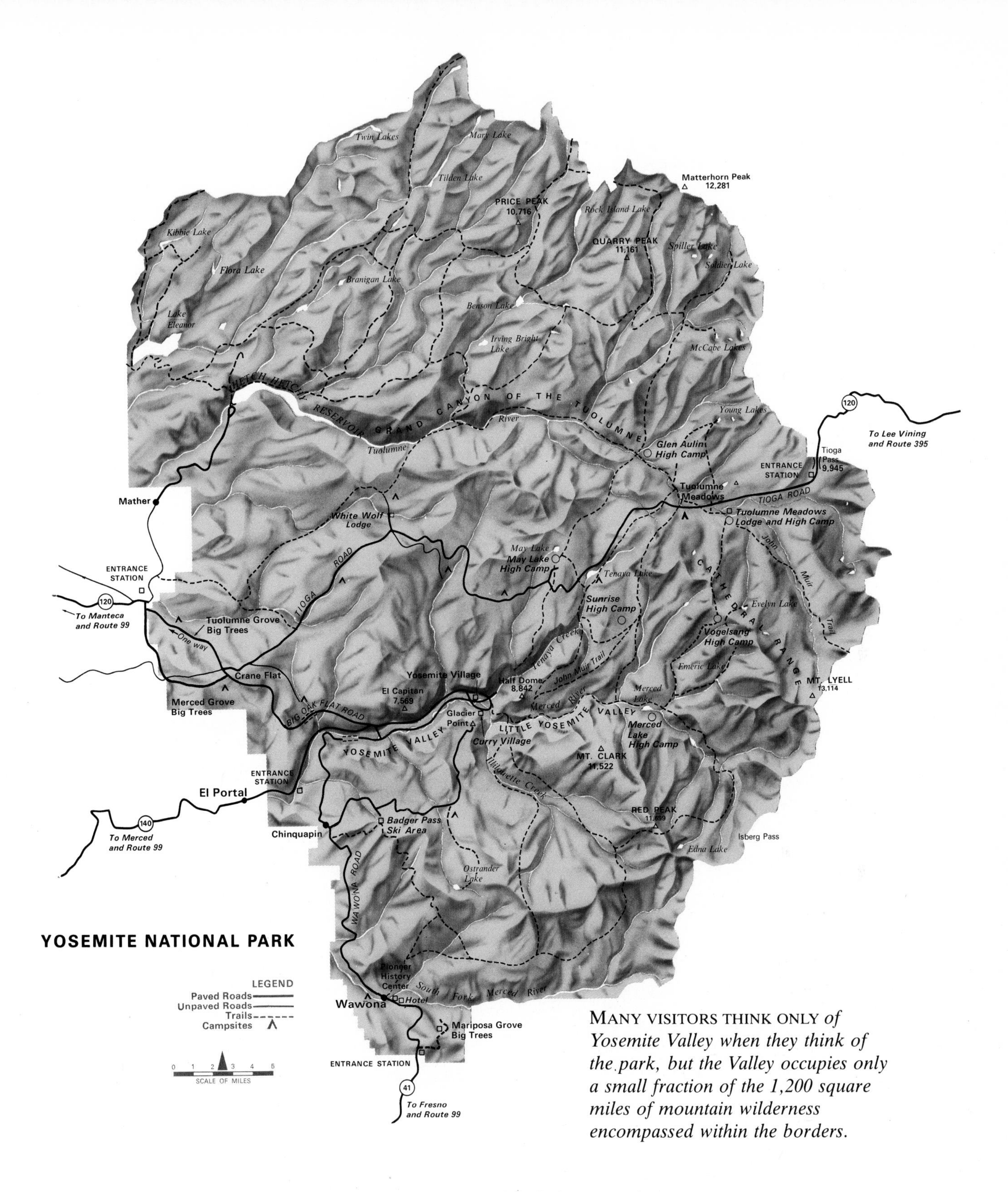

MANY VISITORS THINK ONLY *of Yosemite Valley when they think of the park, but the Valley occupies only a small fraction of the 1,200 square miles of mountain wilderness encompassed within the borders.*

LEFT: A DISTINGUISHED PARTY, *guided by John Muir and including President Theodore Roosevelt, pauses before passing through Wawona Tree in Mariposa Grove. Roosevelt's 1903 visit to the park encouraged him to press for protective legislation to save more Big Trees and other valuable natural wonders. The Wawona Tree fell during a late winter storm in 1969.*

The Valley

For well over a century, the fabled grandeur of Yosemite Valley has drawn enchanted travelers to the park. The majesty of the granite cliffs rising above the forested floor, the beauty of the tumbling waterfalls, and the tranquility of the Merced River have combined to mesmerize generations of Americans.

The Valley is a profound gorge, cut by a river and gouged by glaciers, that is 7 miles long, a mile wide, and 3,000 feet deep. Its walls are actually mountain-sized rocks, separated from each other by side canyons. So deep did the glaciers and the river cut into the granite, that they left behind the tributary streams, which cascade from hanging valleys around the rim of the canyon in waterfalls of extraordinary height.

As the central tourist attraction of the park, it is here that most of the recreational opportunities and accommodations are found. All roads into the park end at Yosemite Village. Despite the efforts of the Park Service to shunt visitors to other sections of the park, hordes of tourists pour into the compact canyon on long summer weekends. The congestion partly cancels the value of coming to the park—but it is understandable. Once seen and felt, the Valley becomes a part of the beholder, and it is with reluctance that he settles for anything less.

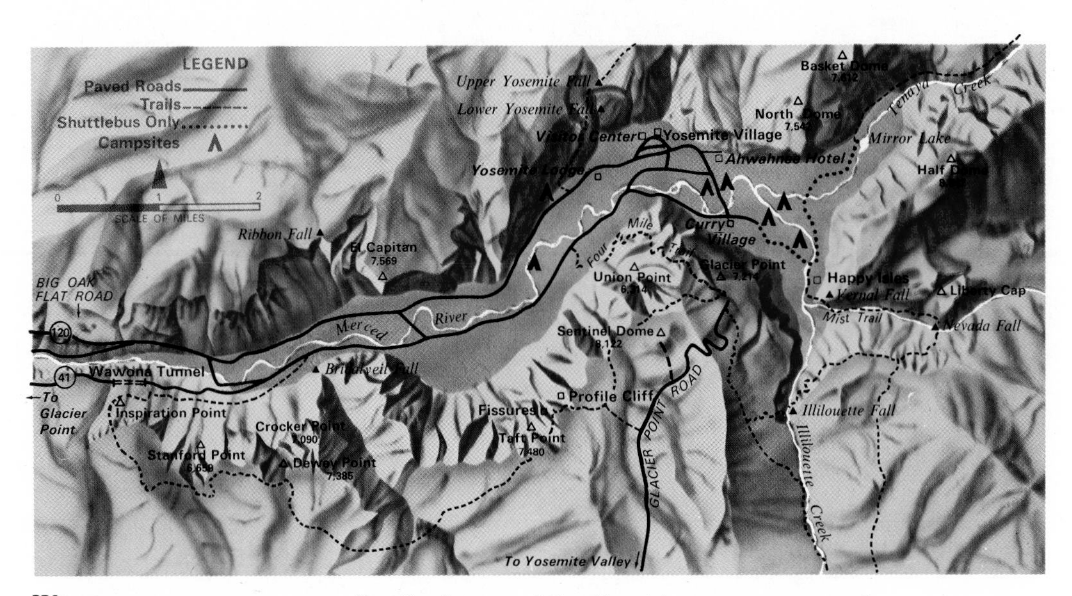

Within a glacial valley *7 miles long and 1 mile wide are concentrated most of the spectacular domes, cliffs, and waterfalls in the park. Here, too, are the major resorts and campgrounds, located along the Merced River.*

Yosemite Falls, *one of the highest waterfalls in the world (2,425 feet), tumbles over the north wall in spring with a vigor that shakes the ground, then wanes to a mere trickle by September.*

David Muench

DAVID MUENCH

AUTUMN FLASHES BRIGHTLY *in Yosemite Valley, helping to relive the somber mood of the conifer forest. Within the Valley is a concentration of broadleafed trees that brings forth a more varied display of fall color than in the Yosemite forest in general. At higher altitudes, off the Tioga Road and the highway to Glacier Point, are groves of aspen that turn to shimmering gold in autumn.*

HOW YOSEMITE VALLEY WAS FORMED

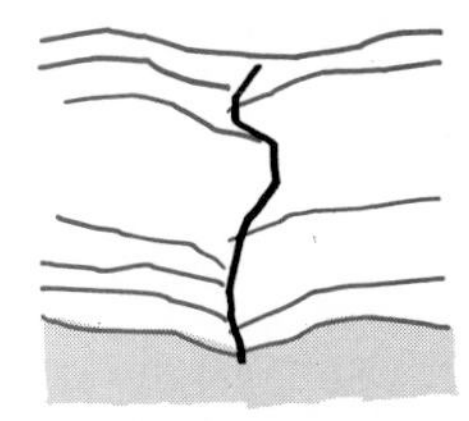

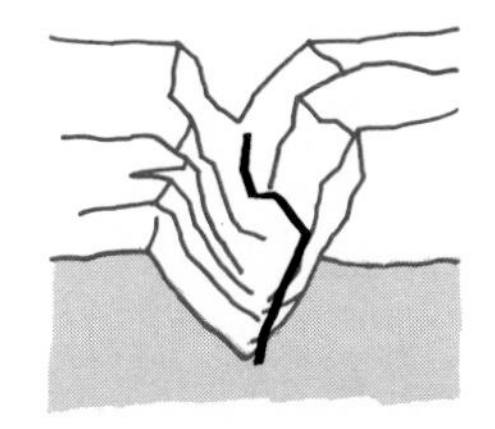

1. BROAD VALLEY STAGE 2. V-SHAPED CANYON STAGE 3. GLACIAL STAGE 4. POST-GLACIAL STAGE

GLACIERS FORMED YOSEMITE VALLEY *during the Ice Age. 1. First, the land now occupied by the Sierra was covered with low ridges, rolling hills, and broad valleys. The ancestral Merced River flowed gently. 2. A gradual upheaval tilted the Sierra block, causing the sluggish Merced to rush seaward, carving a 2,000-foot, V-shaped canyon. 3. A change in climate caused ice to accumulate in the high country. In time, glaciers gouged the valley to U-shape and rounded the peaks to domes. 4. The glaciers advanced and receded three times, then melted and left a lake dammed behind the terminal moraine. Eventually, the lake dried up, leaving the level floor of today's meadows.*

THERE ARE FISH *in the Merced River, but you'll have more success in the back country. The river is high in early summer when it is fed by the runoff from mountain streams, then it calms to a meandering stream for the remainder of the summer.*

RICHARD ROWAN

MALCOLM LOCKWOOD

LARGER THAN THE ROCK OF GIBRALTAR, *El Capitan stands sentinel at the lower end of the Valley. Said to be the largest single block of granite in the world, its sheer cliff attracts rock climbers.*

TED STRESHINSKY

BEST WAYS TO EXPLORE *Yosemite are to hike the trails or bike the roads. For a wet but-close up view of Vernal Falls* (LEFT), *hike the 1.4-mile Mist Trail up from the Valley floor.*

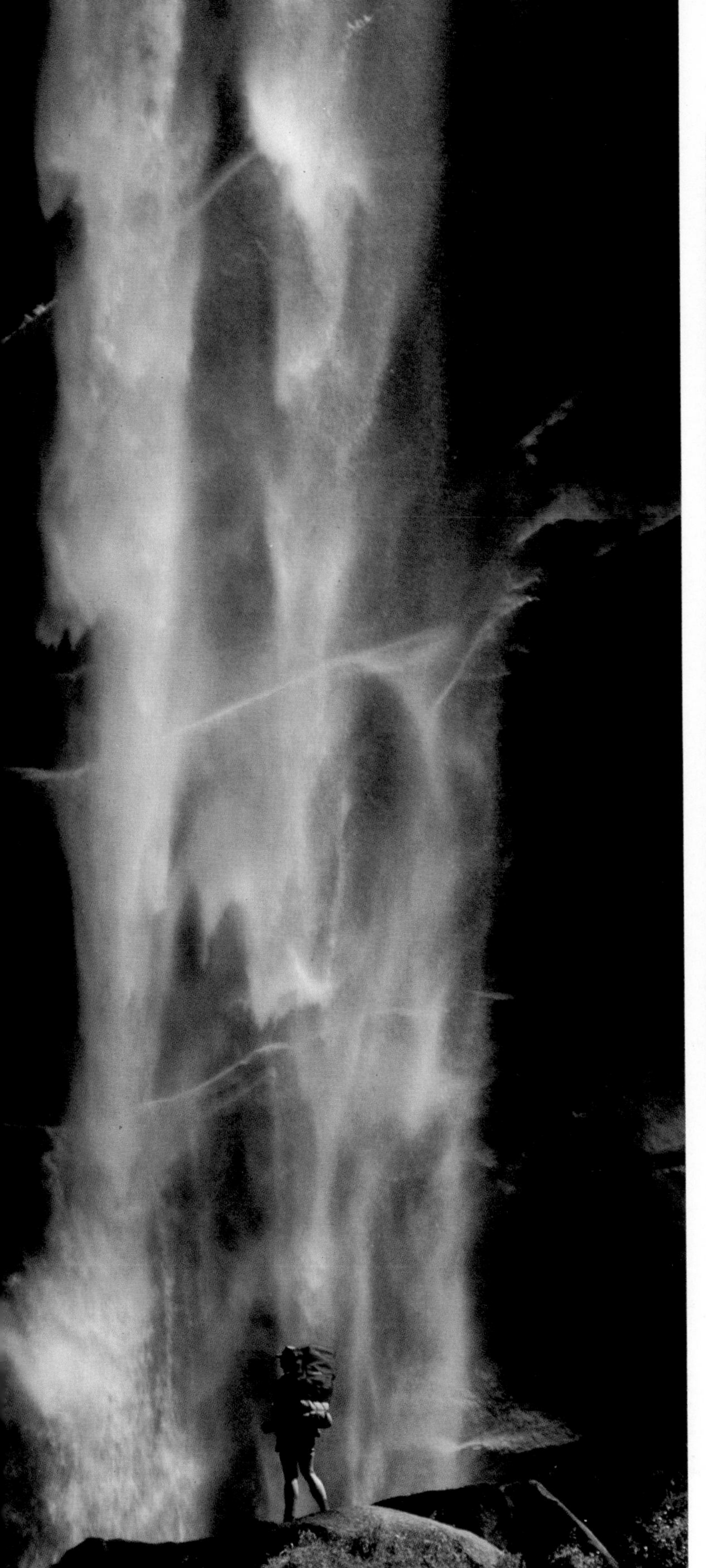

TED STRESHINSKY

A TRULY UNIQUE HOSTELRY, *the distinguished Ahwahnee Hotel has long been a stopping place for American presidents, foreign dignitaries, and other travelers who have delighted in the grand scale of its architecture and its spectacular location at the base of the cliffs on the north side of the Valley.* ELLIOTT VARNER SMITH

RANDY MORGENSON

"THE GRAND WINTER STORMS," *wrote John Muir, "seldom set in before the end of November. The fertile clouds, descending, glide about and hover in brooding silence, as if thoughtfully examining the forests and streams with reference to the work before them."*

North Country

NORTH OF YOSEMITE VALLEY, a 700-square-mile province of forest, rivers, and mountains spreads to the boundaries of the park. This is a land of solitude, of fresh and unspoiled country, inviting and accessible alike to hiker, camper, and motorist. Traversed by a single east-west highway, which crosses the highest pass (9,941 ft.) of any road in the state, the area is spotted with campgrounds and laced with trails that radiate from beautiful Tuolumne Meadows.

It was from the north that the first wagon road penetrated to the Valley that had become known to the public in the 1850s. Earlier travelers had entered the Valley on horseback, spending 12 saddle-sore hours on the rough trail from Wawona. For 22 years the only access had been by foot or on a horse. Then the Coulterville-Big Oak Flat Road toll road opened in 1874. In 1883, the Tioga Road—a hair-raising mining road that was not completely modernized for 78 years—tied in with it. These old roads, plus the Wawona Road that opened as a toll road in 1875, form the basis of the present intensively used highways.

NATIONAL PARK SERVICE

STAGE PASSENGERS RODE ENVELOPED *in a cloud of dust on the Big Oak Flat Road, a toll road that entered the Valley from the northwest in 1874. The narrow road zigzagged down the north wall of the canyon by a series of switchbacks. Passengers endured 20 hours of jouncing in the ride from the railhead. The toll road operated for 35 years. It was put out of business when a railroad reached El Portal near the park's west boundary.*

GRANITE PEAKS *of the Sierra crest encircle sparkling Tenaya Lake in this view from Olmstead Point. A favorite high country camping spot, the lake, situated along Tioga Road, is one of the few high country lakes that can be easily reached by automobile.*

PHILIP HYDE

IN A WEEK-LONG HIKE, *you can loop five High Camps in the park with refreshing stops by icy streams and sparkling falls like the White Cascade* (RIGHT) *at Glen Aulin. Tents at Sunrise High Camp* (BELOW) *are typical of accommodations—simple, comfortable, but unpretentious. Linen and blankets are supplied, and hearty meals are served family style. You can even enjoy the luxury of a hot shower.*

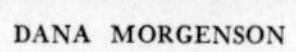

DANA MORGENSON

DANA MORGENSON

TED STRESHINSKY

GATEWAY TO THE NORTH COUNTRY, *Tuolumne Meadows is regarded as one of the most beautiful subalpine meadows in the Sierra. Trails to High Sierra destinations fan out from the meadow, which is itself one stop in the loop of the High Camps.*

NATIONAL PARK SERVICE

ORIGINALLY BUILT IN *1883 as a wagon road to service a mine, the Tioga Road was not completely modernized for 78 years, and driving it was a nerve-racking adventure. For 60 twisting miles, it snaked between trees and boulders, roller-coastered up and down hills, and skirted precipices. Until its realignment in 1961, many miles were still in the same condition as they were in this vintage scene.*

FORREST JACKSON

IN ANY SEASON, *the high country holds the viewer captive. In this mid-January aerial view, a white mantle blankets the land and clouds of snow swirl off North Dome in the foreground. Across Tenaya Canyon is famed Half Dome. In late June, at 6,000 feet, shooting stars* (ABOVE) *brighten a wet meadow near Crane Flat.*

FORREST JACKSON

South of the Valley

In the richly diversified area south of the Valley, most of the main attractions are located right on the highway.

Climbing out of the Valley, the road pauses at a turnout for a last sweeping view of the canyon, then winds upward through conifer forests. At Chinquapin, the Glacier Point Road branches off. It passes Badger Pass, a crowded ski center in winter and a quiet wildflower park in summer, and ends at the tip of Glacier Point, a breathtaking overlook 3,200 feet above the floor of the Valley.

South of Chinquapin, the main highway passes through bucolic Wawona. One of the earliest settlements in the park, Wawona was the location of an overnight rest stop known as Clark's Station from 1857 to 1874. The Wawona Hotel that serves the public today opened in 1879. Nearby is the park's prime historical exhibit: a frontier village recreated from pioneer buildings gathered from all over the park. Finally, the road sidetracks to the cathedral-like groves of Big Trees.

FORREST JACKSON

ICICLE-DRAPED VIEW *greets the traveler emerging from the east portal of Wawona Tunnel in this view taken just before sunset on a mid-January day.*

ELLIOTT VARNER SMITH

GINGERBREAD BUILDINGS *of the Wawona Hotel, though modernized, look basically the same today as they did when they were built in 1879 and 1917. Grazing deer, only mildly interested in the intruding photographer, contribute to the bucolic atmosphere.*

FORREST JACKSON

FROM GLACIER POINT, *a breathtaking sweep of Yosemite high country, diffused with what John Muir called "good-night alpenglow," spreads to the horizon under a mountain sunset. Two great glacial canyons sweep around Half Dome and enter the Valley: to the left, Tenaya Canyon; to the right, the Little Yosemite, through which the Merced River flows, down Nevada and Vernal falls.*

ROLF ZILLMER

A TENACIOUS JEFFREY PINE *on the top of Sentinel Dome, a mile from Glacier Point, draws its sustenance from cracks in the granite. This lightning-scarred and stunted tree is a favorite subject of photographers. In a forest, the Jeffrey grows straight and tall, ranging from 60 to 170 feet. Cross-country skiers* (RIGHT) *can choose from more than 50 miles of trails in the park. The slopes at Badger Pass challenge beginning and intermediate downhill skiers from mid-December to early April.*

RICHARD ROWAN

JOSEF MUENCH

GNARLED GRIZZLY GIANT *in the Mariposa Grove is the fifth largest of the Sierra Big Trees. Latest estimates place its age at 2,700 years. It still grows as fast as trees half its age.*

SEQUOIA AND KINGS CANYON

PARK FACTS: *Location:* Southeastern California. *Discovered:* Sequoia, 1853; Kings, 1845. *Established:* Sequoia, September 25, 1890; Kings, March 4, 1940. *Size:* Sequoia, 630 sq. mi.; Kings, 717 sq. mi. *Altitude:* Sequoia, 1,700 to 14,495 ft.; Kings, 4,600 to 14,242 ft. *Climate:* Summers hot; winters snowy. *Season:* All year, but some main roads closed by snow. *Annual visitors:* Sequoia, 973,400; Kings, 869,900. *Accommodations:* Motels, cabins, campgrounds (some all-year and snow camping). *Activities:* Tours (Crystal Caves), hiking, horseback riding, skiing (Wolverton). *Information:* Supt., Sequoia/Kings Canyon National Parks, Three Rivers, CA 93271.

THE TWIN PARKS, SEQUOIA AND KINGS CANYON, located next to each other on the ridgepole of California, are administered as one and share many features in common.

Within the boundaries of each are several thousand acres of sequoias, the largest trees on earth. Each park encompasses a hikers' domain of spectacular peaks and canyons, threaded with an intricate trail system. The two parks are accessible to the same highway on the west, and they share the opposite ends of one of the most spectacular roads in the park system, the Generals Highway, that runs along the shoulder of a mountain ridge and reveals sweeping views of high mountains and deep valleys.

SEQUOIA, THE SECOND OLDEST NATIONAL PARK, was established in 1890 as a sanctuary of 252 square miles to protect the largest remaining sequoia groves from the logging destruction that had befallen their larger and more accessible neighbors.

The trees were considered a species of the genus (also containing *Sequoia sempervirens*, the coast redwood) which had been named for Sequoyah, inventor of the Cherokee alphabet. The giant sequoia (common name), Big Tree (poetic and unmistakable), Wellingtonia (British), Sierra redwood (Forest Service) are one and the same: *Sequoia gigantea*, which most authorities are now giving a new, unmusical name, *Sequoiadendron giganteum.*

The largest tree (by volume) in the world, the sequoia is a relic of a preglacial genus that was once distributed over much of the world. During the Ice Age, glaciers swept away all but the few stands in the Sierra that had been

MYSTIC BEAUTY *of the Big Trees impresses most visitors as much as does the size and age of the magnificent sequoias. Few other trees possess such powers of enchantment.*

DAVID MUENCH

SAVE-THE-REDWOODS LEAGUE

SEQUOIA NATIONAL PARK *is named for the great redwood trees which in turn were named for a Cherokee Indian, Sequoyah (ca. 1760-1843), who invented an alphabet of 86 characters for his tribe and taught his fellows to read and write. His deeds so impressed the Austrian botanist who named the redwoods that he registered the trees under the name* sequoia. *In Cherokee language, the name had an odd meaning: as nearly as it can be translated, it meant "neither this nor that" and it was appropriately applied to the opossum.*

growing on land higher than the obliterating ice. These residues of a once-encompassing forest now constitute the groves that are mostly within the protection of the two national parks and adjoining national forests.

Extensive as the present-day groves appear to be, nothing that can be seen today begins to match the vast sequoia forest that was still intact just a century ago. Between 1862 and 1900, logging operations wiped out the finest forest in the world, containing at least two trees—and possibly four or more—that must have been bigger than the world's largest tree, the General Sherman in Sequoia's Giant Forest. Ironically, two of these giants were not cut for their wood, but simply so that sections of their trunks could be exhibited at two world's fairs.

At an early date, public-spirited citizens and conservationists became alarmed by the rapidity with which lumbering activities were destroying the Big Trees. One of the last straws was the building of a sawmill about 9 miles from the Giant Forest, as part of an ill-fated cooperative colony. Determined action resulted in creation of the national park that placed the trees under permanent protection. President Harrison signed the bill creating Sequoia National Park on September 25, 1890. Established at 252 square miles, the park was enlarged over the years to its present 630.

For 24 years after the park was established, it was administered by the Army. Congress did not appropriate sufficient funds to support a resident administration, and the development of facilities and trails was entrusted to cavalry units that served in the park during the summer months. The troops withdrew each fall and left the area open for 9 months of poaching, trespassing, and illegal grazing. In time, adequate sums were appropriated, and the park administration was taken over by civilian administrators in 1914. Under the direction of a sequence of able and dedicated superintendents and enlightened concessioners, the park has been developed with integrity and naturalness.

SIERRA BIG TREE
(*Sequoiadendron giganteum*)

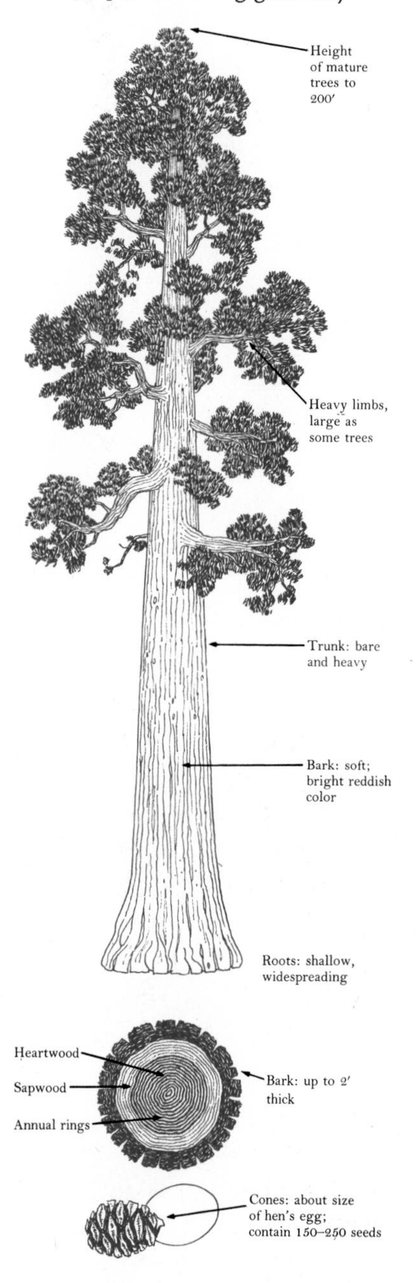

TWO KINDS OF REDWOODS *grow in California, one along the coast, the other in the Sierra. Though not of the same species, the two are often compared. The Big Tree* (Sequoiadendron giganteum) *is not as tall as the coast redwood* (Sequoia sempervirens), *but is more massive, has thicker bark and heavier, more angular limbs; its cones are larger, needles scalier.* RIGHT: *Winter snowfalls deepen the silence in the cathedral-like groves.*

RUSSELL LAMB

High Country

For nine months of the year, the high country in Sequoia and Kings Canyon national parks belongs to the native wildlife; during the other three, this roadless domain is a playground for a varied lot of devotees, some hiking alone, some in small groups, and some in organized parties.

The main traffic arterial is the John Muir Trail, which begins in Yosemite Valley and runs south for 225 high-elevation miles to Whitney Portal, about half of its route lying within the boundaries of Kings Canyon and Sequoia parks. This remarkable pathway, which took 40-odd years to complete, was first conceived by the Sierra Club in 1892. Its route was surveyed over several years, construction was begun in 1915, and it was finally finished in 1938. The trail was named in honor of John Muir, who died just before construction was started.

A network of supplementary trails within the two parks gives access to the full variety of High Sierra terrain: cool, silent forests of fir and pine; knife-edged passes; snowbanks; hundreds of lakes; marshy alpine meadows sprinkled with wildflowers; and talus slopes where marmots sun themselves.

RANDY MORGENSON

DAVID MUENCH

AN EXHILARATING MOMENT *is experienced by these backpackers on the northeast ridge of Big Pine Canyon as they look to the distant Palisades and Kings Canyon.*

MAN'S TOUCH *on the high country, a sturdy marker guides hikers on the trail network. In early summer, ice cones still cover the ground at this trail junction in Sequoia National Park. Kern Ridge cuts the horizon in the distance.*

IN A LAND OF SUPERLATIVES, *it is not surprising to see not one, but two rainbows forming twin arcs over McClure Meadow in Kings Canyon National Park after a summer shower.*

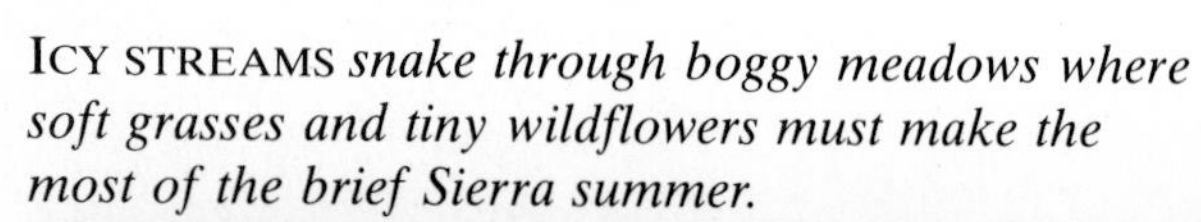

ICY STREAMS *snake through boggy meadows where soft grasses and tiny wildflowers must make the most of the brief Sierra summer.*

RANDY MORGENSON

RANDY MORGENSON

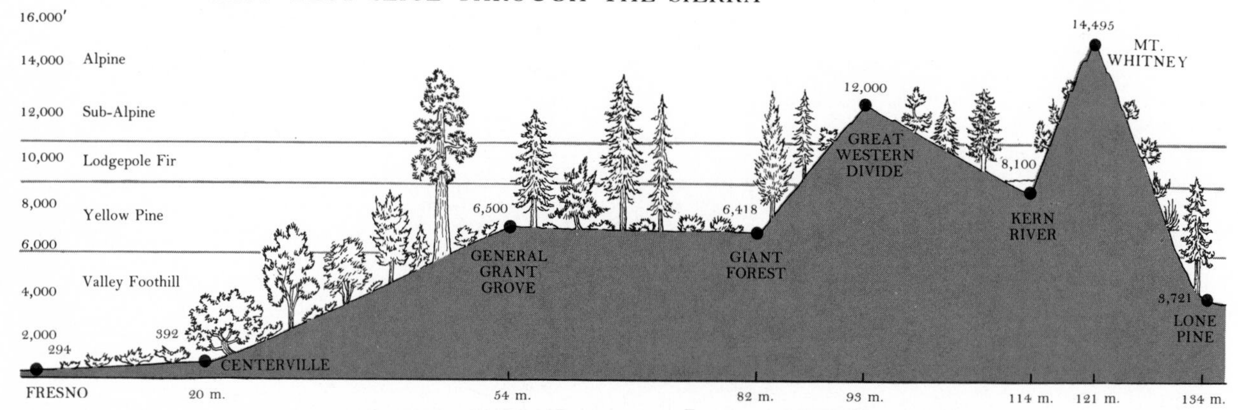

EAST-WEST SLICE THROUGH SEQUOIA *reveals the extreme range of altitude, terrain, and tree-cover encompassed within the park's boundaries. In a span of 67 miles, the elevation ascends 8,000 feet to the top of Mount Whitney on the eastern border, then drops 11,000 feet in a brief 13 miles.*

RANDY MORGENSON

IN A DEEP GROOVE *worn by the passage of thousands of hikers and pack animals over the years, the John Muir Trail swings across typical high country in Upper Basin, Kings Canyon. Where such trails are located near lakes, streams, and alpine meadows, they are being relocated to prevent erosion, overgrazing by pack animals, and changes in the ecological balance.*

RUSSELL LAMB

EASTERN SIERRA VIEW, *photographed from near Lone Pine, takes in lofty Mount Whitney (at right), highest peak in the continental United States outside of Alaska. The 14,495-foot peak was named for J. D. Whitney, leader of the Geologic Survey party that first determined its height, in 1864. The snowy peak at left in the photograph is 12,944-foot Lone Pine Peak.*

IN A SETTING OF MOUNTAIN GRANDEUR, *Evolution Lake lies below the sharp 13,117-foot peak of Mount Huxley and the snowfields of Goddard Divide in this view from the slopes of Mount Darwin in Kings Canyon National Park.*

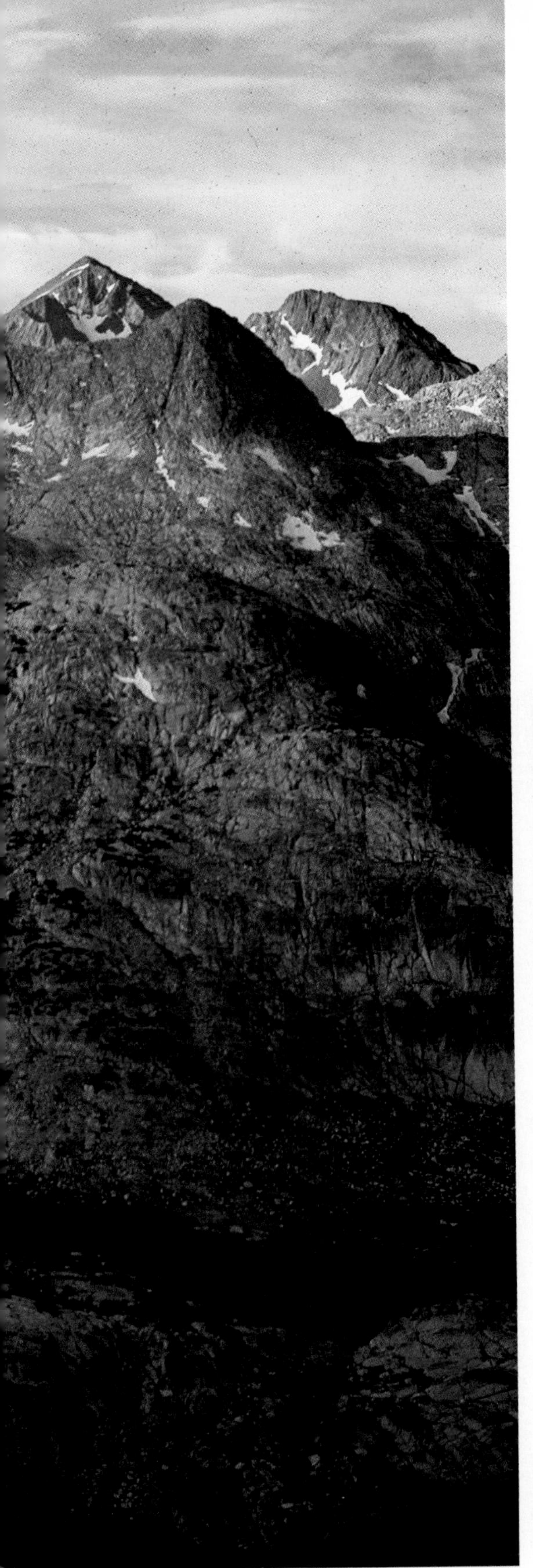

JOSEF MUENCH

PHILIP HYDE

SHOWY ALPINE FIREWEED *thrives on a rocky slope near Granite Pass.*

CHANNEL ISLANDS
(proposed park)

A KIND OF AMERICAN GALAPAGOS

PARK FACTS: *Location:* Offshore southern California between Santa Barbara and San Pedro. *Discovered:* 1542 by Spanish explorers; explored in 1800s. *Established:* Anacapa and Santa Barbara made national monument, 1938; San Miguel administered by National Park Service; these islands plus Santa Cruz and Santa Rosa being considered for national park status, 1980. *Size:* 22 sq. mi. *Altitude:* Sea level to 930 ft. *Climate:* Temperate, some fog, and strong winds on San Miguel. *Season:* All year. *Annual visitors:* 56,100. *Accommodations:* Primitive campgrounds, East Anacapa and Santa Barbara. *Activities:* Boating (no moorings, need skiff to land), diving, fishing, guided archeological tours (San Miguel). *Information:* Supt., Channel Islands, 1699 Anchors Way Dr., Ventura, CA 93003.

CHANGE IS IN THE WIND for five of southern California's eight offshore Channel Islands. At press time, a bill before Congress would unite Anacapa, Santa Barbara, San Miguel, Santa Rosa, and Santa Cruz islands into a national park. Anacapa and Santa Barbara, the two tiniest islands (about 700 acres each) achieved national monument status in 1938; San Miguel Island, long part of a Navy target range, is managed by the National Park Service with limited public visitation by permit only. Santa Rosa and Santa Cruz are mostly in private ownership but under the new bill portions could be managed by the Park Service.

Volcanic remnants of an ancient mountain range, the islands were separated from the Santa Monica Mountains by extensive earthquake activity some 500,000 years ago. Today only eroded peaks jut from the sea.

The Channel Islands were among the first parts of California to be explored by Europeans. Cabrillo anchored near Anacapa in October 1542; in 1769 Portola made reference to it in his log. Chumash Indians inhabited the islands until the 1800s; San Miguel has a large number of midden and village sites, particularly important because of their antiquity. Later, sheepherders grazed flocks and cultivated parts of Santa Barbara Island, but lack of fresh water discouraged these attempts. Until 1956, a semi-hermit, "Frenchy" LeDreau, resided on Anacapa. He and his hut are gone, but Frenchy's Cove, Anacapa's best anchorage, and Frenchy's Cave are testimonials to his tenancy.

Most familiar to boaters and fliers, these intriguing islands on the horizon now invite hikers and campers to view a kind of American Galapagos. Here, canyons and meadows support plants and wildlife found nowhere else. Beaches and rocky inlets are refuges for seals, sea lions, and sea elephants. They are surrounded by teeming sea life, visible to scuba divers and snorkelers, and provide a grandstand seat for the annual gray whale migration.

AUTOMATED LIGHT *warns ships away from rocky shores of East Anacapa Island.*

RALPH CLEVENGER

ROBERT C. GILDART

PROUD PROBOSCIS *proclaims elephant seal's arrival on shore* (LEFT). *Visitors can get a good view of these large mammals from many of the islands and at the same time seek the shy gray island fox* (BELOW LEFT). *The sea teems with life below the surface. Tide pools expose anemones, urchins, and starfish. Divers off Santa Barbara Island find large concentrations of tiny, twisting brittle stars* (BELOW) *on the sandy channel bottom.*

ROBERT C. GILDART

RALPH CLEVENGER

NATIONAL PARK SERVICE

TEMPORARY ISLAND DWELLERS, *these pinnipeds haul out on the shores to mate and give birth. San Miguel Island plays host to more species than any other single location in the world.*

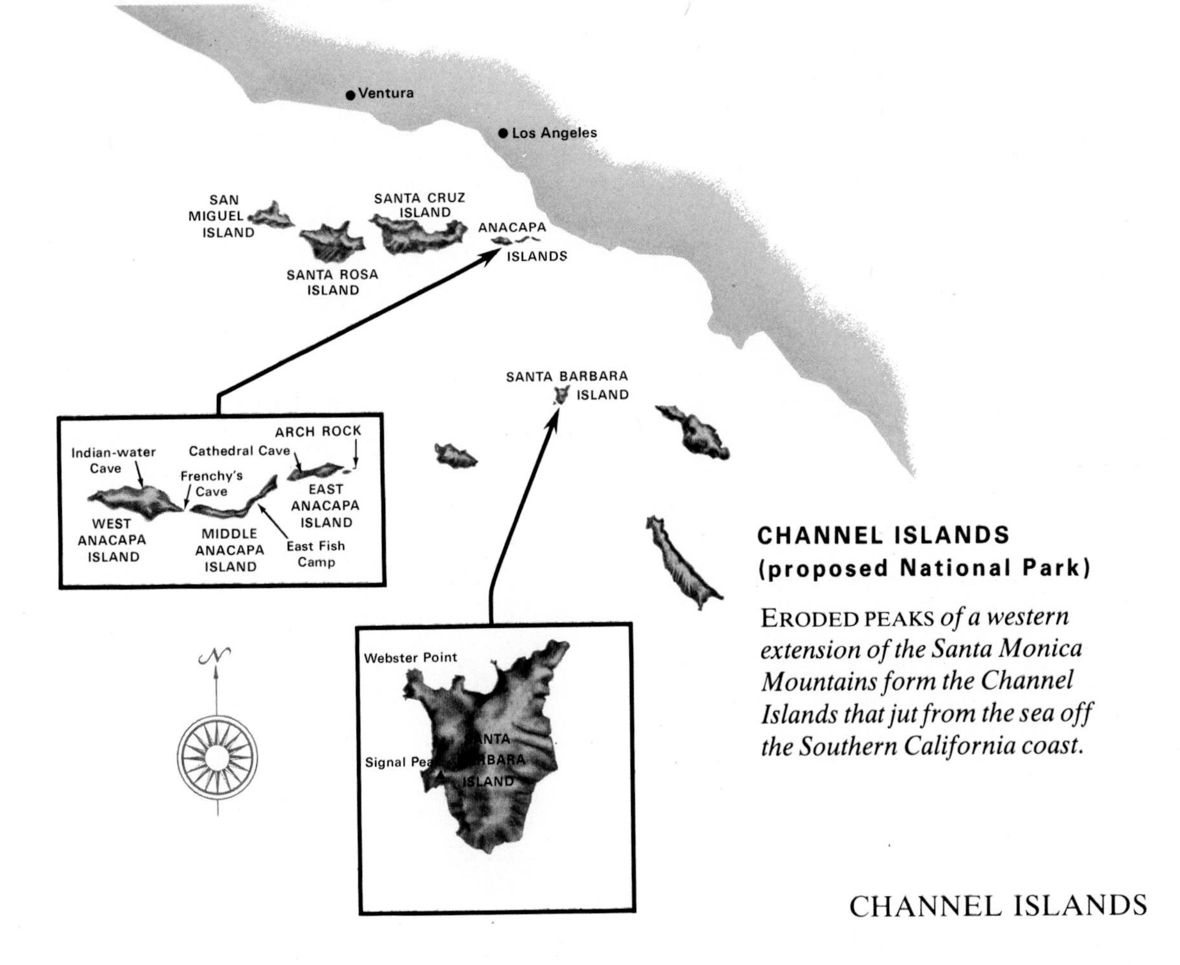

CHANNEL ISLANDS (proposed National Park)

ERODED PEAKS *of a western extension of the Santa Monica Mountains form the Channel Islands that jut from the sea off the Southern California coast.*

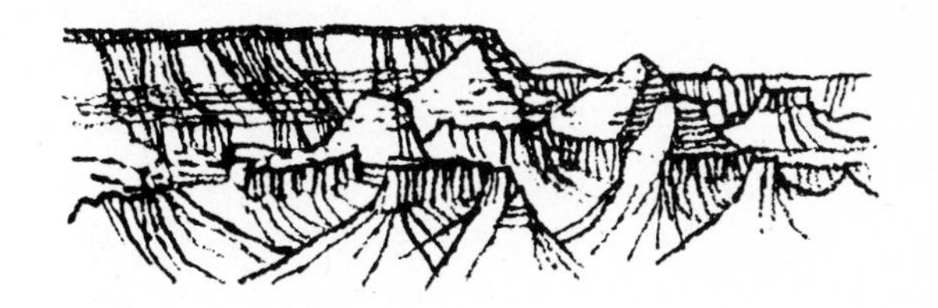

GRAND CANYON

THE STORY OF THE EARTH ITSELF

PARK FACTS: *Location:* Northwestern Arizona. *Discovered:* 1540. *Established:* February 26, 1919. *Size:* 1,100 sq. mi. *Altitude:* 1,200 to 9,165 ft. *Climate:* Progression of climate from that of Mexican desert at canyon bottom to that of S. Canada at North Rim. *Season:* South Rim, all year; North Rim, mid-May to mid-October. *Annual visitors:* 2,986,200. *Accommodations:* Lodges, campgrounds. *Activities:* River rafting, mule tours, hiking, biking, bus tours, flightseeing. *Information:* Supt., Grand Canyon, AZ 86023.

FROM EITHER NORTH OR SOUTH, you approach through rather flat, temperate country full of the familiar, friendly things of field and forest. The land is broken occasionally by picturesque minor gullies. Then, at the sudden edge of the Grand Canyon of the Colorado, you are confronted with one of the most sublime spectacles of this planet. Yet, standing on the brink for the first time, your impulse may be to turn away. It is not any fear of height, nor of the incredible wilderness gap in a land otherwise subdued by civilization. Rather it is disbelief, even saturation with the incredible size of it all.

A little knowledge of the canyon begets a craving for more. A great knowledge of it begets a greater craving for more. When you look into its depths you are looking back some twenty million centuries. Nowhere else can you do so. Nowhere else is geologic history, beginning with the oldest exposed rock on earth, so clear and orderly. When you look into the gorge you look over a bewildering array of plants and animals that in less awesome surroundings need this whole continent to find suitable homes.

Nobody has seen all of the Grand Canyon—and soon it may be too late to try. Human exploitation of the canyon has accelerated rapidly over the past century, and the builders of dams are eager to bend an already reduced Colorado River ever more to their purpose.

"Ours has been the first, and will doubtless be the last, party of whites to visit this profitless locality," reported Lieutenant J. C. Ives, exploring the Grand Canyon region in 1857. Ives was no historian, and he was an even worse prophet. Thirteen men of Coronado's Spanish expeditions had entered the region in 1540, and the captain in command of the party had registered official dismay at the

AUTUMN COMES EARLY *on the North Rim. Usually by the first of September, crisp nights have tinged aspen leaves a lively yellow, highlighted by dark green firs at the canyon's edge.*

JOSEF MUENCH

unbridgeable barrier posed by the chasm. Since Lieutenant Ives' cheerless pronouncement, the canyon has yielded profit in varying degrees to ranchers, miners, prospectors, horse thieves, hermits, and bootleggers, and has been visited by millions of parties of tourists.

In large measure, the Grand Canyon owes the beginnings of its fame as a natural wonder to the explorations of a one-armed major of artillery named John Wesley Powell. In 1869, the dauntless major set out with a small party in four boats to run the length of the Green River and the Colorado as far as the bottom of the Grand Canyon. It was a bucketing ride that cost the major two of his boats and collapsed the nerve of three men in the crew. But he prevailed. He proved the canyon explorable. The accounts of his adventure are still to be read today. River-runners, in fact, use his journals as a guide to their own journeys.

The results of Powell's turbulent dash included widespread publication of accounts of the adventure. These led to greater awareness of the region, and this in turn led to much further exploration of a Southwest that was, before Powell, largely left blank by the map makers. Subsequent expeditions by Powell and others achieved two great results: Several branches of natural science found fertile new fields for study, and Powell's enhanced reputation won him the directorship of the fledgling Smithsonian Institution, which he put well on the way to its present eminent station.

This focus of attention also produced great optimism about the immediate tourist value of the Grand Canyon. Around 1880, an ex-miner named John Hance improved upon the Indian trails to some degree and upon the truth to an even greater extent to impress visitors. By the turn of the century there were hotels, tourist camps, orchards, and gardens at various levels all the way down to the river, and several aerial tramways across it. The Santa Fe Railroad built a spur line from Williams to the South Rim in 1901 and the El Tovar Hotel three years later, but for most operators the optimism proved short lived. The resorts failed, one by one; cable cars rusted in their moorings; the neglected trails disappeared (John Hance's name survives only on a few minor landmarks). For many years, only the Santa Fe and the Fred Harvey Company were able to make a go of the tourist business, and the canyon was left mostly to the Indians whose homes were in the canyon and along its rims (many of the Havasupai continue to live at the bottom of the great gorge). In time, substantial interests invested in tourism, and the park has for years served as a magnet for tourists.

Efforts to preserve the canyon as a national park were begun soon after the establishment of Yellowstone but required 30 years of campaigning to take effect. The first protagonist, Senator Benjamin Harrison of Indiana, introduced a bill in the upper house in 1882 to make the area a national park. It failed. It was not until 1893 that Harrison, as President of the United States, was able to establish the Grand Canyon Forest Preserve, which could be and was exploited by mining and lumber interests. President Theodore Roosevelt took up the cause after his visit in 1903. He established Grand Canyon National Monument in 1908. An act of Congress in 1919 established Grand Canyon National Park.

WESTERN WAYS

"WE ARE SWEPT BROADSIDE DOWN, *and are prevented, by the rebounding waters . . . in these billows, and are carried past the danger." Powell wrote in 1869 of such scrapes again and again, and one was captured by his artist, R. A. Muilerse.*

KOLB STUDIOS

ON JACOB'S LADDER, *a turn-of-the-century party of riders descends toward the river on mule and horseback. The trail is no longer used, and neither are horses, but other trails still lure explorers into the canyon depths.*

WESTERN WAYS

ALTHOUGH HANDICAPPED *by the loss of an arm in the Civil War, ex-artillery major John Wesley Powell daringly led an expedition down the unexplored Colorado River in four boats in 1869. Photographed 22 years later, he still looked hale and hearty, ready for further exploits.*

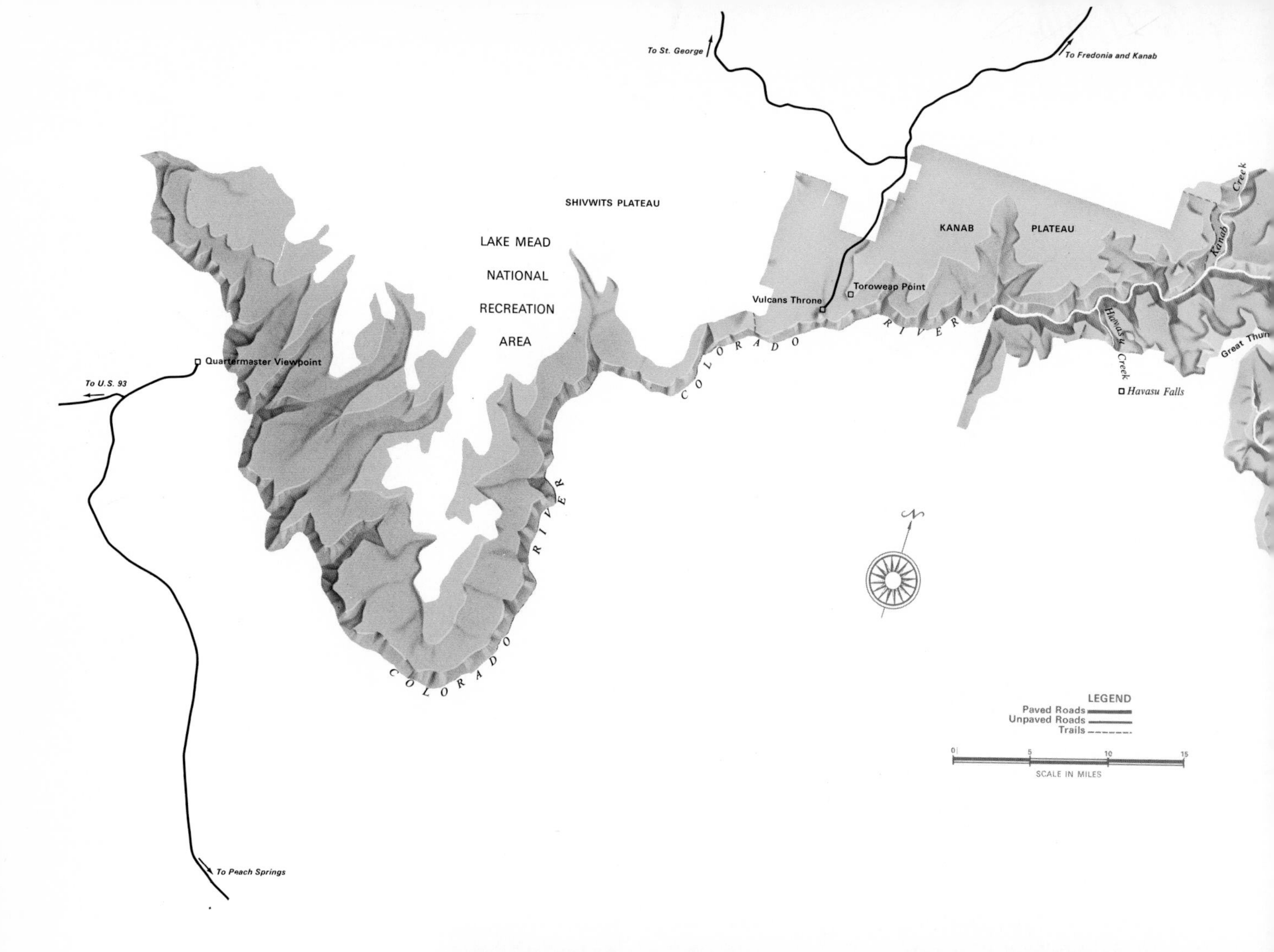

CARVING A SINUOUS WAY *through brown Tapeats sandstone, crystal-clear Deer Creek hastens to its 125-foot fall into the Colorado River.*

DAVID MUENCH

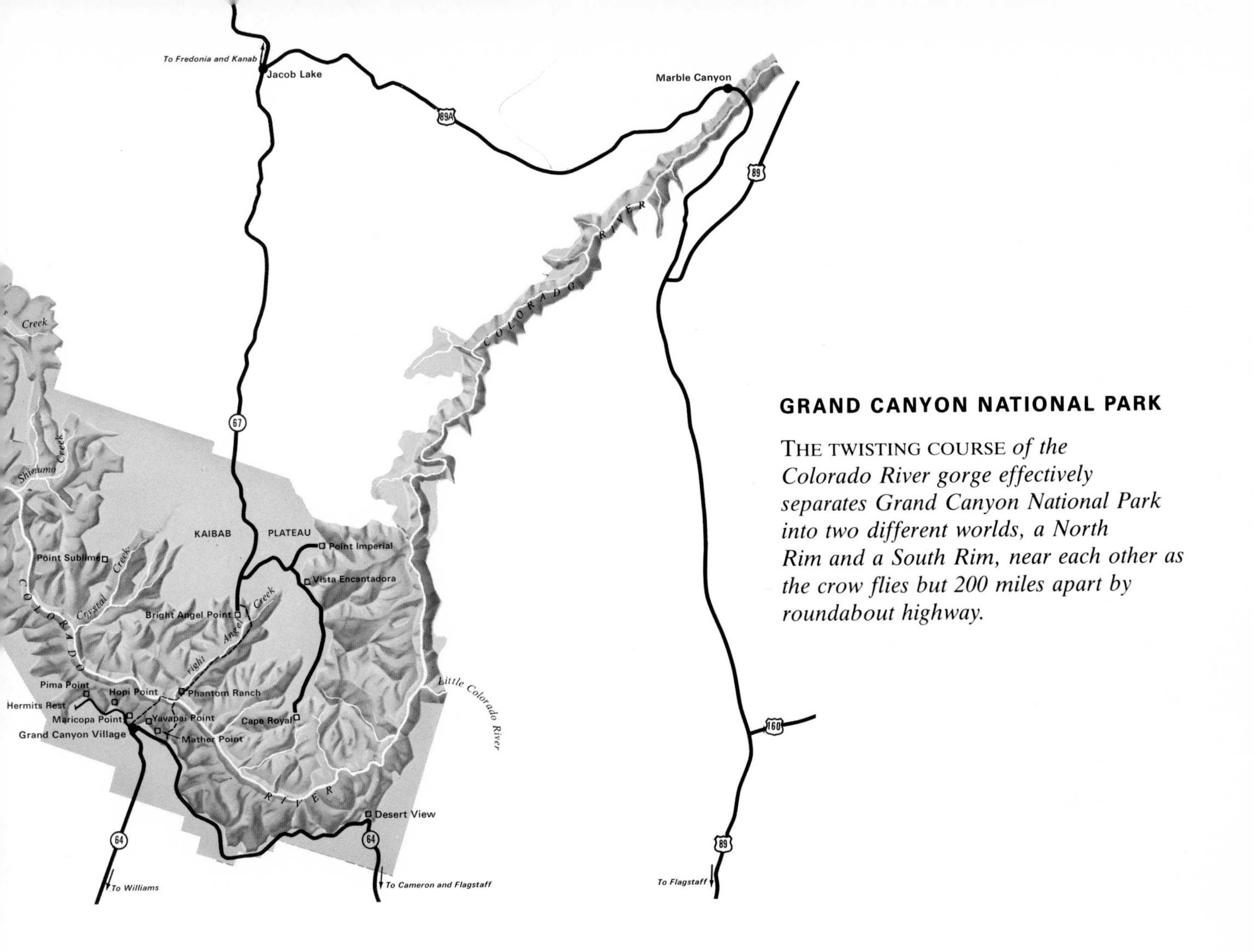

GRAND CANYON NATIONAL PARK

THE TWISTING COURSE *of the Colorado River gorge effectively separates Grand Canyon National Park into two different worlds, a North Rim and a South Rim, near each other as the crow flies but 200 miles apart by roundabout highway.*

HOW THE GRAND CANYON WAS FORMED

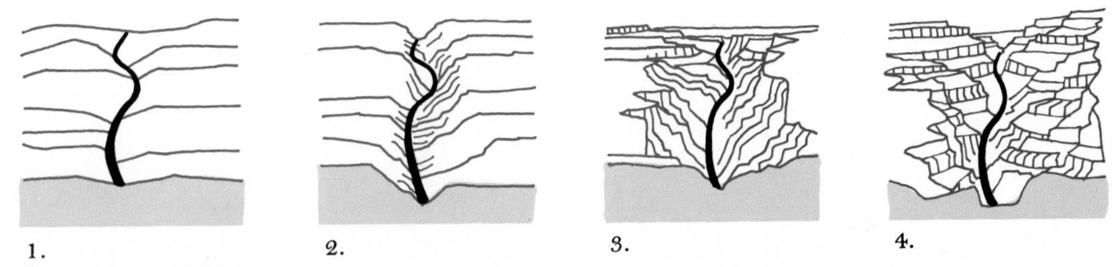

CARVED BY THE SAME FORCES AS A ROADSIDE GULLY, *the Grand Canyon is an awesome example of the work of erosion. 1. First, a lazy river meandered through a gently sloping plain, cutting a shallow channel into the earth. 2. Pressure within the earth slowly uplifted the surface, causing the river to run faster, cut deeper. As the channel deepened, land on both sides was gradually eroded into the river and the canyon took on a V shape instead of forming a straight-sided trench. 3. Sides of the V-shaped canyon began to break down as forces of erosion attacked them. Rain sluiced soil down into the canyon bottom where it was carried away by the river. Water from melting snow froze in cracks in rocks, splitting them and further crumbling canyon walls. 4. Over the ages, the river continued to cut deeper, ever following its original configuration, and as it cut, the break-up of the canyon walls became accelerated, disintegrating in an ever-widening gap. In time, the canyon wall may disappear, leaving a flat plain again.*

COMPETING WITH STRIKING COLORS *of the canyon walls, a delicate rainbow arcs through a foreboding sky in this dramatic view from Pima Point on the South Rim.*

BILL DANIELS

WEATHER WATCHING *is a major part of a Grand Canyon experience. The eerie light cast over the canyon when a storm is imminent presents a particularly awesome scene.*

BILL DANIELS

GRAND CANYON
History of the Earth

I In the rocks, two billion years.

Possibly, the first spark of life on earth came to be while the rock of the Vishnu Schist formed the surface of this region, instead of the bottom layer of the Grand Canyon.

This black rock of the inner gorge is some of the oldest man has seen on this planet. Its age is two billion years, an incomprehensibly long span. The youngest rocks in this canyon, only 280 million years old, were deposited as sand by an encroaching sea long before the first dinosaur roamed the land.

The story is written in layers deposited so tidily that geologists use the canyon as a primer. There are missing chapters. Nothing remains of the Ordovician and Silurian geologic periods, which followed the Cambrian, and there is very little left of the Devonian period, which came after the Silurian and before the Carboniferous.

Later chapters are written at Bryce and Zion.

II Down the canyon walls, a continent's range of life.

What is in the rock tells a long story. What is on it does too, in miles rather than time.

A sturdy hiker can go down to the bottom of the Grand Canyon and back out again in two days. The experience lets him see plant and animal life that he could also see by walking from Mexico's Sonoran desert to the shore of Hudson's Bay in Canada.

The great depth of the canyon plays tricks with temperatures and precipitation to such a degree that the local range of climate equals the natural range of the entire continent. Mostly, the life zones occur in their logical order; but in some sections, the desert is higher than the Canadian zone, where the canyon's topography makes a high area hot and a lower one cool.

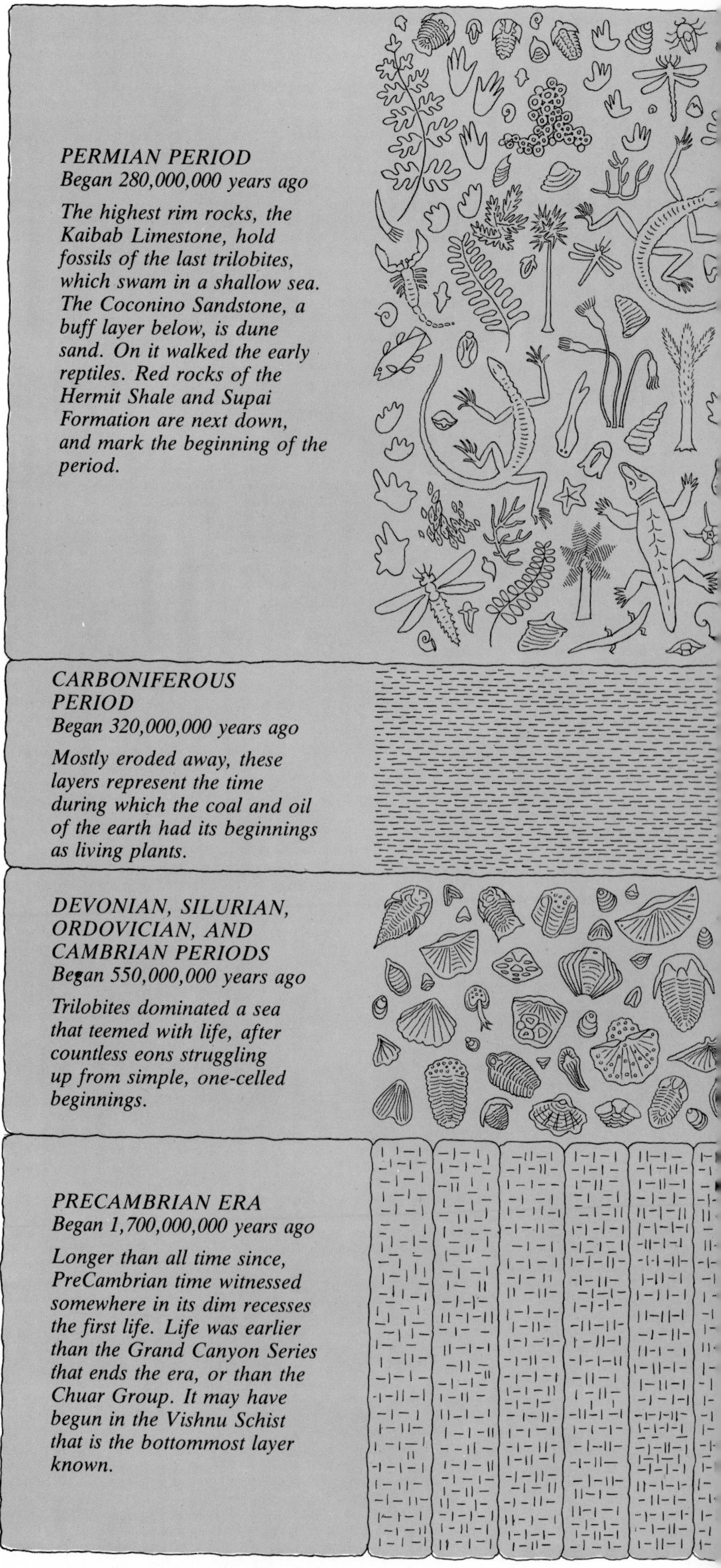

PERMIAN PERIOD
Began 280,000,000 years ago

The highest rim rocks, the Kaibab Limestone, hold fossils of the last trilobites, which swam in a shallow sea. The Coconino Sandstone, a buff layer below, is dune sand. On it walked the early reptiles. Red rocks of the Hermit Shale and Supai Formation are next down, and mark the beginning of the period.

CARBONIFEROUS PERIOD
Began 320,000,000 years ago

Mostly eroded away, these layers represent the time during which the coal and oil of the earth had its beginnings as living plants.

DEVONIAN, SILURIAN, ORDOVICIAN, AND CAMBRIAN PERIODS
Began 550,000,000 years ago

Trilobites dominated a sea that teemed with life, after countless eons struggling up from simple, one-celled beginnings.

PRECAMBRIAN ERA
Began 1,700,000,000 years ago

Longer than all time since, PreCambrian time witnessed somewhere in its dim recesses the first life. Life was earlier than the Grand Canyon Series that ends the era, or than the Chuar Group. It may have begun in the Vishnu Schist that is the bottommost layer known.

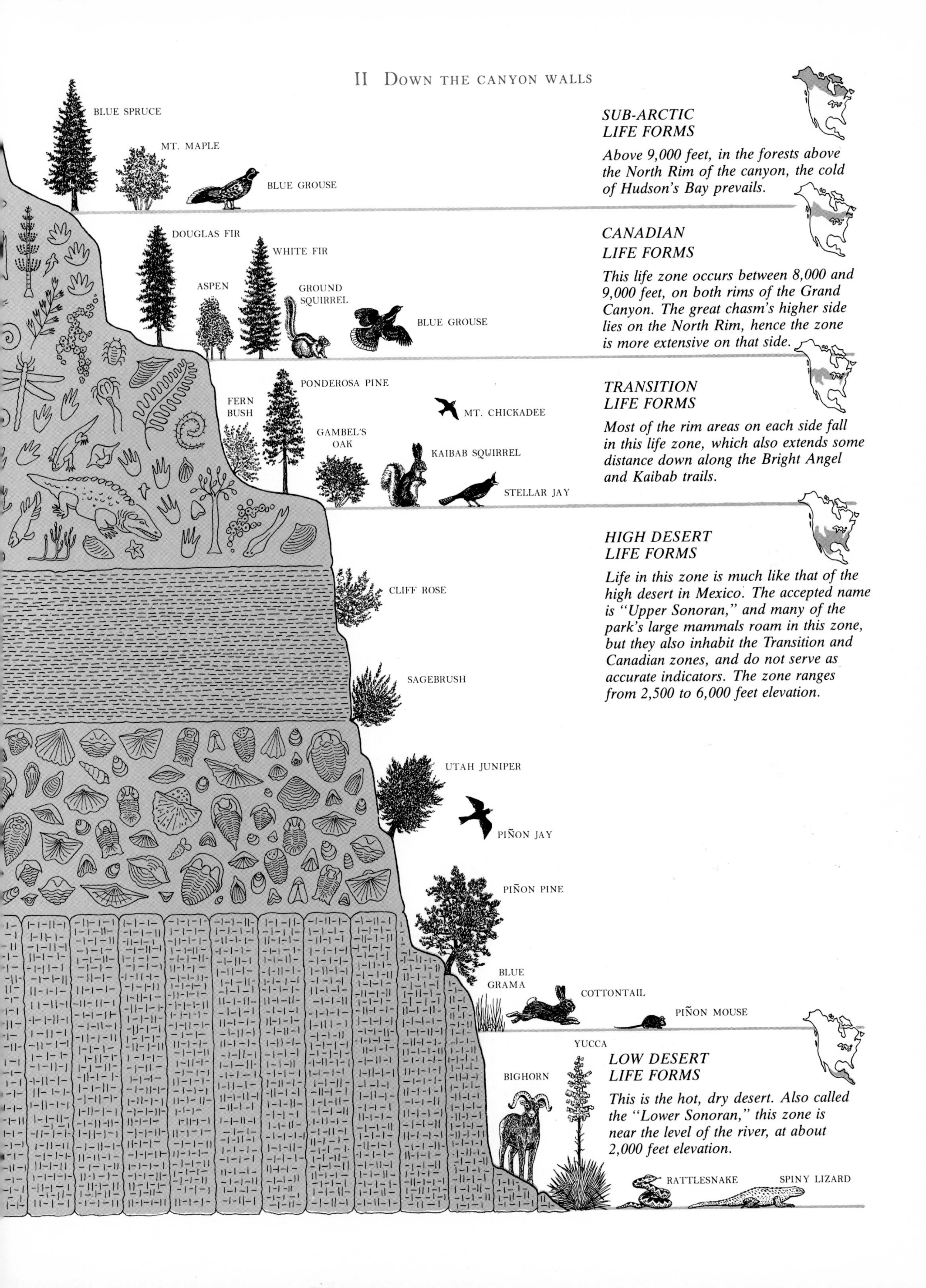
II Down the canyon walls
BLUE SPRUCE
MT. MAPLE
BLUE GROUSE
SUB-ARCTIC LIFE FORMS
Above 9,000 feet, in the forests above the North Rim of the canyon, the cold of Hudson's Bay prevails.
DOUGLAS FIR
WHITE FIR
ASPEN
GROUND SQUIRREL
BLUE GROUSE
CANADIAN LIFE FORMS
This life zone occurs between 8,000 and 9,000 feet, on both rims of the Grand Canyon. The great chasm's higher side lies on the North Rim, hence the zone is more extensive on that side.
PONDEROSA PINE
FERN BUSH
MT. CHICKADEE
GAMBEL'S OAK
KAIBAB SQUIRREL
STELLAR JAY
TRANSITION LIFE FORMS
Most of the rim areas on each side fall in this life zone, which also extends some distance down along the Bright Angel and Kaibab trails.
CLIFF ROSE
SAGEBRUSH
HIGH DESERT LIFE FORMS
Life in this zone is much like that of the high desert in Mexico. The accepted name is "Upper Sonoran," and many of the park's large mammals roam in this zone, but they also inhabit the Transition and Canadian zones, and do not serve as accurate indicators. The zone ranges from 2,500 to 6,000 feet elevation.
UTAH JUNIPER
PIÑON JAY
PIÑON PINE
BLUE GRAMA
COTTONTAIL
PIÑON MOUSE
YUCCA
BIGHORN
LOW DESERT LIFE FORMS
This is the hot, dry desert. Also called the "Lower Sonoran," this zone is near the level of the river, at about 2,000 feet elevation.
RATTLESNAKE
SPINY LIZARD

South Rim

There are two centers of tourist interest in the park—the North Rim and the South Rim of the great canyon. They are a mere 10 miles apart to a crow, or two days' hard hiking to one of stout heart and strong limb, or 215 road miles distant from each other. A great many enchanted visitors prefer to see one rim one year, the other the next.

"No matter how far you have wandered hitherto, or how many famous gorges and valleys you have seen, this one, the Grand Canyon of the Colorado, will seem as novel to you, as unearthly in the color and grandeur and quantity of its architecture, as if you had found it after death, on some other star." So wrote John Muir, after he had visited the South Rim in the 1890s, eloquently summarizing the emotional response that this vast spectacle evokes in the traveler when he first sees it.

It is at the South Rim that the great majority of travelers experience this emotional impact. For nearly a century, tourists have converged here to soak in the unbelievable view. Being closer to major population centers and trunk highways than its counterpart across the canyon, the South Rim is easily accessible by bus, plane, or car, and it has always drawn the heavier volume of tourists. As a consequence, it is well provided with facilities for travelers both inside and outside the park. Even in winter, when snow is deep on the ground but not on the plowed roads, the South Rim is accessible and the visitor can enjoy the unforgettable sight of the canyon walls frosted with snow.

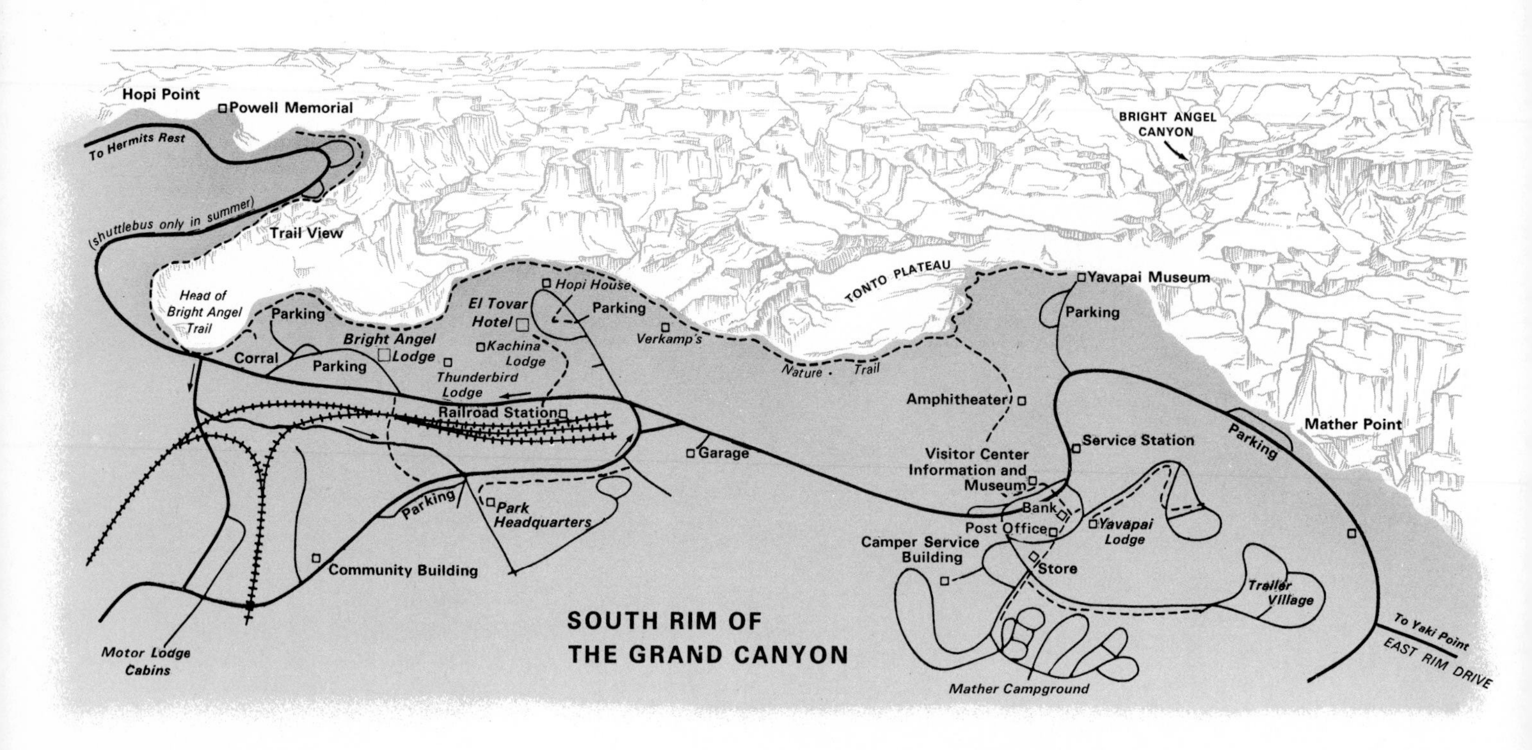

JOSEF MUENCH

OPEN ALL YEAR, *the South Rim shows a very different face when snow mantles the higher elevations. Though most facilities are closed, the dramatic view of the canyon in this quiet mood draws many visitors who feel that this is the time when the canyon is at its best.*

JOSEF MUENCH

STARK SHAPES AND BRILLIANT COLORS *fill the canyon in an afternoon of intense sunlight. In the softer light of morning, the views from the South Rim are colored in pastel hues of blue, purple, and gold. On a stormy day, the canyon becomes dark and moody; then in the misty brightness following the storm, it glows with a fresh softness.*

North Rim

On the North Rim, altitudes run a thousand feet or so higher than on the South Rim. Snow falls early and deep. The end of the tourist season is in sight by October, when the aspens put on a great, golden show of color. When the snow flies, as many as 200 inches may blanket the ground by May. Then warming updrafts from the canyon encourage wildflowers to bloom just at the rim. As snowbanks melt before a warming sun, the bright flowers spread ever more widely. Flowers fill meadows that are still ringed with snowbanks near the forest's edge.

CURIOUS BUT CAUTIOUS *mule deer seem to be waiting for the photographer to make the first move. Most commonly seen of the park's large animals, they appear often on both North and South rims.* G. C. KELLEY

RUSSELL LAMB

STANDING ON THE BRINK *of the canyon, visitors are inevitably awed by the incredible spectacle that spreads out before them. At several points, paths lead to fenced view points at the very edge of the canyon wall. The view to the opposite wall is awesome; the view down, dizzying.*

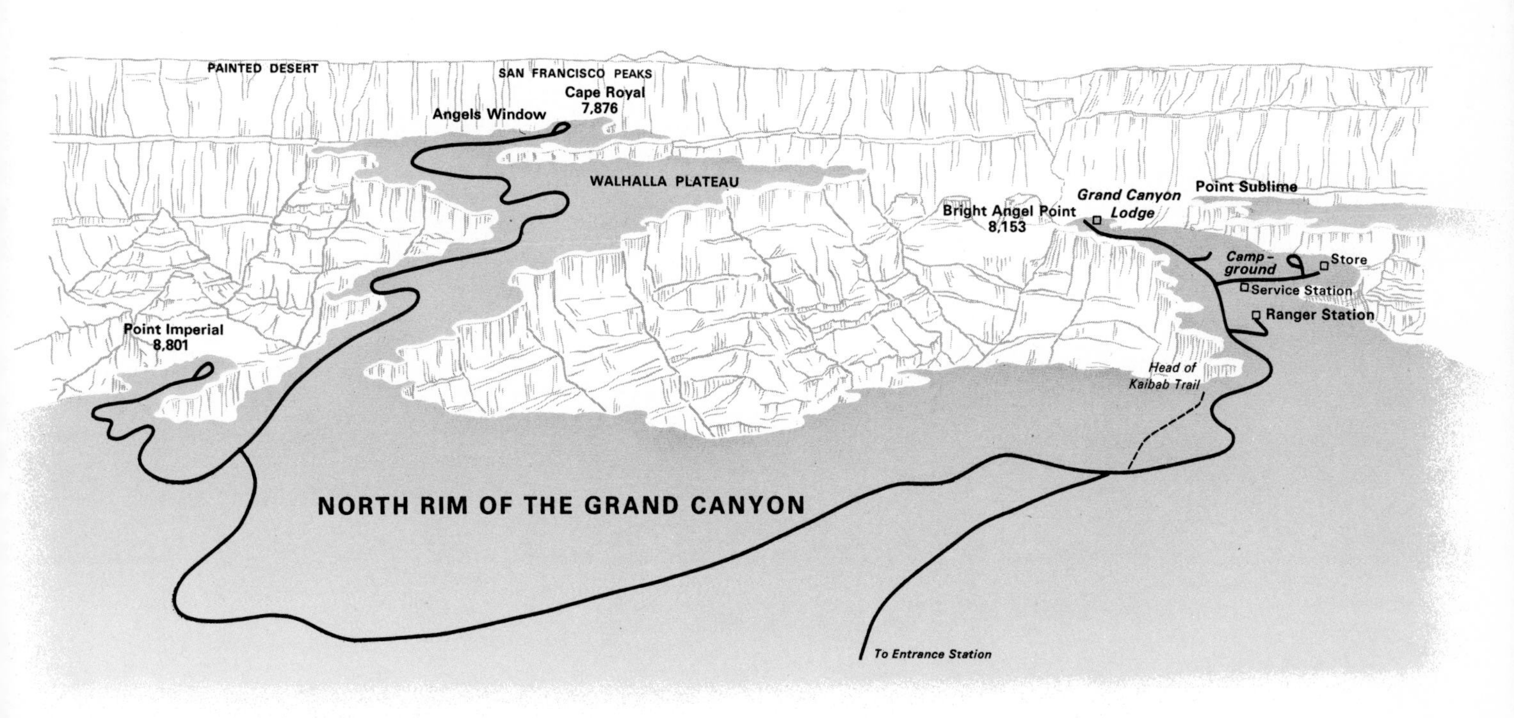

DARWIN VAN CAMPEN

ON THE LOFTY NORTH RIM, *flaming autumn colors light the quaking aspens after September. Beyond, for as far as the eye can see, the canyon and its many side canyons provide pastel contrast to the vivid display on the rim.*

Inner Canyon

IF YOU PAUSE FOR AN HOUR OR TWO somewhere along the rim and let the Grand Canyon soak into your soul, you will feel some of the lure that turns men into explorers. You will get enough of the big view and will want to get a closer look at the working parts. Sooner or later you will be tugged down one of the trails into the inner canyon.

From either rim, you can hike down to the river. From the South Rim, mule trips go to the bottom of the canyon via the Bright Angel and Kaibab trails; from the North Rim, they descend as far as Roaring Springs (less than halfway down) via the North Kaibab Trail. In summer, the methodical beasts plod their memorized routes in such numbers that a certain air of the barnyard arises from the wide, sun-drenched trails. Users of this service will gain a new appreciation of the width of a mule.

At the bottom of the canyon is a desert, hot and dry and relieved only by the river. It is no place for Sunday strollers to wander aimlessly. Hikers should carry plenty of water and allow two days to get from the rim to the river and back.

JOSEF MUENCH

IN THE DEPTHS OF THE CANYON, *this suspension bridge carries parties across the Colorado to Phantom Ranch. The bridge is part of the Kaibab Trail that descends from both rims.*

ROLF ZILLMER

TO SEE THE RIVER CLOSELY, *visitors must either descend the zigzag trails from the rims or "run" the river by boat. River trips vary in length from 3 to 18 days. From the South Rim, you can ride a mule in one day to Plateau Point or in two days to Phantom Ranch. Mule trips from the North Rim take you only as far as Roaring Springs (9 miles round trip).*

JOSEF MUENCH

ZION

"YOSEMITE VALLEY IN COLOR"

PARK FACTS: *Location:* Southwestern Utah. *Discovered:* 1776. *Established:* November 19, 1919. *Size:* 230 sq. mi. *Altitude:* 3,650 to 8,740 ft. *Climate:* Hot summers, mild winters. *Season:* All year. Facilities closed but main road open in snowy months. *Annual visitors:* 1,308,000. *Accommodations:* Lodge (mid-May through mid-October), campgrounds. *Activities:* Hiking, guided horseback rides, guided bus trips. *Information:* Supt., Zion National Park, Springdale, UT 84767.

ZION CANYON IS A COLORFUL JEWEL set in a land famed for color. It is a serene canyon, majestic with sandstone cliffs which at times rise more than 3,000 feet above its floor. Without the color—the delicate pinks and reds and whites of the sandstone and the fresh green of the cottonwoods, ash, and maples that border the river—these walls and domes might be overpoweringly stern. But the color softens the scene and casts a special aura over the canyon.

Zion has been called a Yosemite done in oils, for without color the sheer cliffs would resemble the California park in many ways. Zion Canyon is a narrow, curving gorge, 8¾ miles long; the upper end is so narrow that two men standing abreast can touch both walls with their outstretched arms. The canyon is cut by the Virgin River, a Jekyll-and-Hyde sort of stream that is usually clear and peaceful, reflecting the cliffs in its calm pools. But a storm in the higher country can transform it into a relentless torrent, tearing savagely at its banks, and carrying boulders and trees like pebbles and twigs.

Such storms are not frequent, but when they come they have their rewarding aspects. Visitors present at such a time will marvel at the power of the river and perhaps be loath to turn their eyes from the racing waters. But during a hard rain, a look up the walls of the canyon reveals waterfalls springing to life and plunging over the usually dry cliffs, some dropping 2,000 feet in a single leap. More than 50 large waterfalls and hundreds of smaller ones have been counted at one time during a heavy rain. It has been estimated that each year the Virgin carries three million tons of sediment from the park—an average of 180 carloads each day. Thus the river works as it has worked for centuries, cutting the canyon deeper and deeper through the strata of stone.

TOLD IN THE ROCKS OF ZION *is the geological story spanning more than 200 million years. The remains of a great ancient desert, this fine example of cross-bedded Navajo sandstone has been shaped by the erosive forces of water, wind, and frost.*

DAVID MUENCH

An excellent road traverses the canyon along the bank of the river and terminates at the Temple of Sinawava. Glorious in daylight hours, the Temple is even more impressive in the soft light of the moon.

There are many good trails, some that penetrate delightful side canyons and others, more strenuous, that climb to the rim on either side. One of the most popular and beautiful is the mile-long walk along the river beginning at the Temple of Sinawava and ending at the entrance to The Narrows. Here the trail passes the Hanging Gardens, where water trickles down the wall to moisten the flowers, ferns, and vines that trail from cracks in the rock.

Zion is an all-year park and each season has its own charm. Spring is fresh with flowers and new foliage. During the hot summer the park is its busiest. In autumn the trees glow brilliantly and tongues of red and yellow flame seem to creep up the ravines. Winter snows seldom linger in the lower part of the canyon, but in the upper portions, a fresh fall converts the landscape into a white fairyland.

Zion was for many years a retreat and a place of special reverence for the Mormon pioneers, who discovered the canyon and named the region "Zion," meaning "the heavenly city of God," and bestowed religious names on many of the rock formations. The area had been originally explored by Spanish padres in 1776, explored 50 years later by Jedediah Smith and his fur-trappers, and then developed by the Mormons a decade after the founding of Salt Lake City in 1847. The area was not set aside for public use until 1909, when it was designated Mukuntuweap National Monument. Ten years later it was enlarged and changed to Zion National Park.

BETTY RANDALL

BRILLIANTLY COLORED *maple leaves are a change from the great sandstone masses and steep canyon walls that form much of the park's scenery. Wooded areas thrive along the Virgin River that flows through Zion Canyon.*

WEEPING ROCK *sheds its tears on visitors who step into the cave behind the falling water. Surface water on the rim seeps down through porous cliffs and emerges as a curtain of falling drops. Seepage is evident throughout the park, and dozens of waterfalls spring to life after a rain.*

ED COOPER

SO TORTURED *is the Zion terrain that it was not completely mapped until 1930 when it was systematically photographed from the air.*

BETTY RANDALL

A BROWSING MULE DEER *comes out of hiding for a late-day snack. Deer range through the canyons and highlands. Though you're not likely to see mountain lions, bobcats, and coyotes, they, too, are among the park's residents.*

COLOR IN THE CLIFFS *is in the rock itself, the vegetation, surface stains, and lichens. The dominant color is red, derived from iron and manganese in the sandstone.*

ANSEL ADAMS

RUSSELL LAMB

TAKING ON NEW DIMENSIONS, *West Temple receives a light dusting of snow that emphasizes narrow ledges in cliffs that at other times seem almost sheer. Snow falls intermittently from December to March. It melts quickly on the canyon floor but usually remains throughout the winter on the canyon rims.*

BRYCE CANYON

"A HELL OF A PLACE TO LOSE A COW!"

PARK FACTS: *Location:* South central Utah. *Discovered:* 1800s. *Established:* National monument, June 8, 1923; national park, September 15, 1928. *Size:* 56 sq. mi. *Altitude:* 6,600 to 9,100 ft. *Climate:* April to October, warm days and cool nights; winters cold, with snow. Air is thin due to high elevation. *Season:* All year; main road kept open in winter. *Annual visitors:* 680,300. *Accommodations:* Lodge (mid-May to mid-October), campgrounds (May 1 to November 1). *Activities:* Hiking, guided horseback rides, snowshoeing, cross-country skiing. *Information:* Supt., Bryce Canyon National Park, Bryce Canyon, UT 84717.

THE PAIUTE INDIANS CALLED IT "UNKA-TIMPE-WA-WINCE-POCK-ICH," which means Red-rocks-standing-like-men-in-a-bowl-shaped-canyon. Ebenezer Bryce, the canyon's first resident, had a saltier phrase. In his words, it was "One hell of a place to lose a cow!" Both descriptions are accurate.

Bryce Canyon is the result of erosive forces. For millions of years, wind, rain, sleet, and frost have worked relentlessly on the multicolored limestone of this great amphitheater. They have shaped countless columns, spires, walled windows, and figures of every description in soft reds, yellows, oranges, grays, and whites. These fantastic forms, filling a huge half-bowl 15 miles across, defy the imagination—or stimulate it, for here is an astonishing variety of shapes, some grotesque, some beautiful.

Just as the forces of nature created the landscape, so do the vagaries of the day alter it for the viewer. The domes and temples and spires never seem twice the same. With every cloud shadow, with every change of light, with every summer shower, the scene is new, and newly exciting. No matter how familiar one may be with this fairyland of form and color, some new formation of some undetected tone is always to be discovered.

It is possible, if you wish, to see Bryce Canyon National Park by car. A paved road skirts the western rim for 20 miles, terminating at Rainbow Point. You can look into a dozen minor amphitheaters, each with a character of its own. From Rainbow Point unfolds a sweeping view not only of the canyon but of the country beyond. On a clear day you can see the Henry Mountains, 90 miles away, the Tushars, 60 miles to the north, and, 80 miles to the southeast on the Arizona border, Navajo Mountain, sacred home of the Navajo's war god.

A FANTASYLAND *to photographers and nature lovers, the eroded cliffs of Bryce were described in 1876 by an enraptured surveyor as "The wildest and most wonderful scene that the eye of man ever beheld." But to Ebenezer Bryce, the first settler, the canyon was "One hell of a place to lose a cow!"*

RUSSELL LAMB

But to experience the park adequately, to capture its true grandeur and its varied moods, walk or ride into its heart over one of the fine trails. Only in this way can you appreciate the beauty of the formations. The trails vary in length, from 1½ to 23 miles, and in gradient from nearly level to steep (those that lead into the canyon itself).

The colorful formations are geologically young—a mere million years of age. They overlie more ancient rocks of the strata exposed today in the walls of Zion Canyon to the west and Grand Canyon to the south. Thus one can trace a fascinating sequence in earth history from the oldest rocks of Grand Canyon, through the more recent walls of Zion, to the comparatively young strata of Bryce Canyon.

Bryce is an all-year park, and although access to some sections is limited, the road to certain of the major points is kept open throughout the winter. The beauty of the spires and minarets is no less breathtaking when the delicate colors stand out in contrast to a blanket of snow and frost.

Bryce has been a tourist destination only since the automobile made access possible. Before then, the area was familiar only to trappers and farmers, and before them, to the Indians, who lived in nearby caves or entered the canyon to hunt or to gather herbs, seeds, and berries. Trappers visited the locality in the early 1800s, Mormon scouts explored it between 1850 and 1870, and the first awe-struck descriptions of the fantastic landscape came from geologists and surveyors who explored the canyon in the 1870s. The first settler, Ebenezer Bryce, for whom the park is named, pastured cattle in the labyrinth from 1875 to 1880. Small settlements grew up nearby, but the area was too remote from railroads and wagon routes to grow. It was not until the first automobiles began to push their way through the sands after 1915 that the area gained recognition as a potential park. It was made a national monument in 1923 and a year later was established as Utah National Park, a name that was changed to the present one in 1928.

HOW THE ERODED FANTASY WAS FORMED

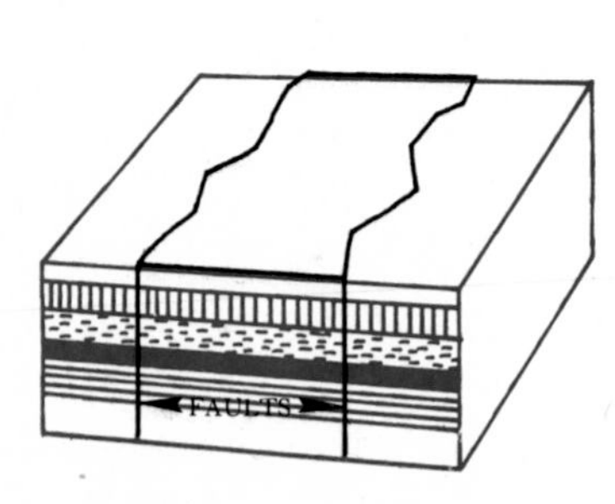

1. DEEP FAULTS *form in earth's crust made of layers of silt, sand, and lime deposited under an ancient inland sea.*

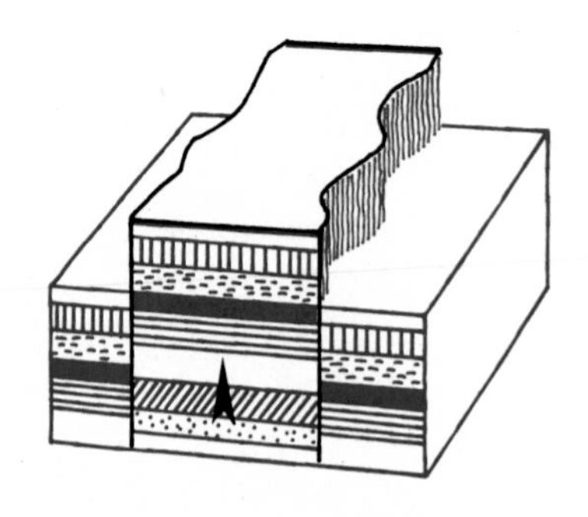

2. MASSIVE PRESSURE *from below slowly forces up block of earth between major faults and forms flat-topped mesa.*

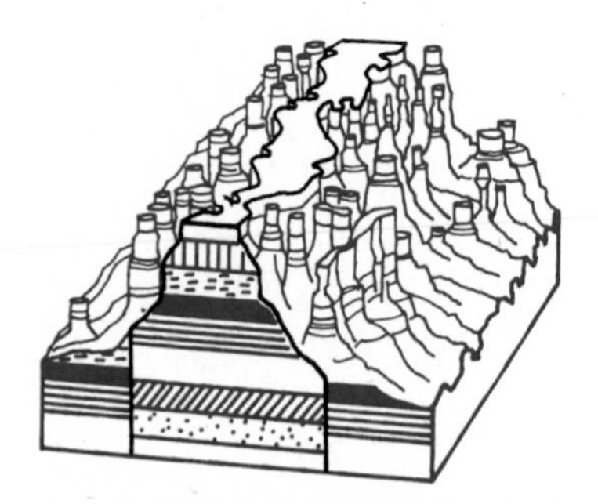

3. RAIN, WIND, AND FROST *action gradually wears away edges of mesa; differences in layers produce odd shapes.*

RENE KLEIN

HIKE THE TRAILS *for close views of the park's strange spires and pinnacles, rock walls, arches, and bridges. If you wish to enjoy the scenery in a less strenuous way, you can view it from overlooks along the rim.*

NATIONAL PARK SERVICE

THE PINK CLIFFS, *considered the finest of Utah's eroded landscapes, stretch for 30 miles along the eastern edge of the Paunsaugunt ("home of the beaver") Plateau. The bright colors, fused into the native rock, are derived from iron—the more iron content, the deeper the red. Bands of different colored and textured rock are layers of ancient sands compressed into rock by the immense weight of the thick layer of earth that once covered them but has long since eroded away.*

DAVID MUENCH

PHILIP HYDE

THIRTY-FOUR MILES *of park roads along the rim and 64 miles of hiking trails above and below it give visitors an opportunity to explore the wonders of Bryce Canyon.*

SHAPED AND RESHAPED *by the elements, all manner of rock formations capture the imagination and seem to take on identities such as "Thor's Hammer"* (LEFT) *on the Navajo Loop Trail.*

SURE-FOOTED MOUNTS *take visitors over trails through the park on three-hour or full-day trips. The Paiutes called Bryce's peculiar rock scenery "Unka-timpe-wa-wince-pock-ich" (red rocks standing like men in a bowl-shaped canyon).*

NATIONAL PARK SERVICE

CAPITOL REEF

SANDSTONE BARRIER TO TRAVEL

PARK FACTS. *Location:* South central Utah. *Discovered:* 1800s. *Established:* National monument. August 2, 1937; park, December 22, 1971. *Size:* 378 sq. mi. *Altitude:* 3,900 to 8,600 ft. *Climate:* Hot in summer, cold in winter. *Season:* All year. *Annual visitors:* 427,700. *Accommodations:* Campgrounds. *Activities:* Hiking, backpacking, jeep tours (from nearby). *Information:* Supt., Capitol Reef National Park, Torrey, UT 84775.

IN THE CANYON COUNTRY OF SOUTHERN UTAH, Capitol Reef is a rugged, harsh land of rocky gorges, soaring arches, and sandstone monoliths. The park encompasses old Capitol Reef National Monument (established in 1937) and large areas north and south of it. At the southern end, the park stretches in a long, narrow corridor to a common boundary with Glen Canyon National Recreation Area.

Waterpocket Fold, a gigantic monoclinal flexure of the earth's crust, extends almost 100 miles down the length of the park and is the up-thrusted "reef" that gives the park half its name. The reef is actually a ridge of sandstone—not a former ocean reef of limestone to which the term more properly applies. But early prospectors called any rocky barrier to travel a reef, and the high, weathered ridge of Waterpocket Fold does indeed create a barrier. The nearly vertical escarpment of the ridge, 1,000 feet high in some sections, presents an almost impenetrable wall to east-west travel across this region.

The erosive action of wind and water against the sandstone barrier of Waterpocket Fold has created most of the scenic splendors of the present park. The brightly colored sandstone layers are gashed by labyrinthine canyons, eroded into natural bridges and arches, or smoothly weathered into great rounded domes. An early visitor fancied that the rounded, buff-colored exposures of Navajo sandstone along the top of the reef resembled a capitol dome; hence the other half of the park's name.

For many park visitors, Capitol Reef is a drive along the highway that crosses the park. But the most rewarding experiences are off the main road. Hiking opportunities vary from easy walks leading to ancient petroglyphs, sandstone tanks (waterpockets), and cliff-top overlooks to wilderness backpacking expeditions. Remote sections of the park are accessible by rough back-country roads.

NARROW CANYONS *lead explorers to hidden crannies and sometimes to a trickling stream or plunge pool brought to this dry land by a summer storm.*

STEPHEN TRIMBLE

STEPHEN TRIMBLE

SETTLED BY MORMON FAMILIES *in 1880, Fruita, now part of the park, was ranch country then. Crops and cattle flourished along the Fremont River. The last resident left in the 1960s, but cattle drives through the park still bring back the feeling of frontier days.*

CAPITOL REEF NATIONAL PARK

A RUGGED LAND *about halfway between Canyonlands and Bryce Canyon, Capitol Reef is cut by only one paved road, but its trails offer fine back-country hiking.*

SEGO LILIES *bloom near Bitter Creek Divide. April, May, and early June are the months to see the park's fruit trees and wildflowers at their best.* BELOW: *The jagged formation of "The Castle" crowns a cliff just north of the Visitor Center.*

STEPHEN TRIMBLE

STEPHEN TRIMBLE

CANYONLANDS

MORE STANDING UP LAND THAN LYING DOWN

PARK FACTS: *Location:* Southeastern Utah. *Discovered:* early 1800s. *Established:* September 12, 1964. *Size:* 402 sq. mi. *Altitude:* 3,800 to 6,000 ft. *Climate:* Hot in summer, cold in winter. *Season:* All year. *Annual visitors:* 86,300. *Accommodations:* Campgrounds. *Activities:* Hiking, jeep tours, float trips, flightseeing (from nearby). *Information:* Supt., Canyonlands National Park, Moab, UT 84532.

CONTAINING "THE MOST VARIED and spectacular examples of erosion in the world," Canyonlands National Park protects a wild array of arches, needles, spires, crenelated mesas, and standing rocks.

The geologic fantasies are the end product of some 20 million years of erosional shaping by two abrasive rivers, the Green and the Colorado, abetted by wind and rain and frost. The multicolored stone is sculptured according to the resistance of its varying layers to the forces of erosion, thereby creating the oddly striped and chiseled abstractions that astound or humble the viewer. The strange forms have stirred men to imaginative namings, such as The Golden Stairs, Elephant Canyon, Island in the Sky, Tapestry Slab, Devils Lane, and Paul Bunyans Potty.

Unlike the narrow, mile-wide chasm of the Grand Canyon downriver, the outer walls of this vast area are 30 to 35 miles apart and the great trough in between is filled with geological oddities that will in another 10 or 20 million years be eroded to flat desert floor.

The park is mostly wilderness, penetrable on foot or horseback or in a four-wheel-drive vehicle. Trails and jeep roads skirt the rim of the high plateaus, plunge down the steep canyon walls (one descent is 40 per cent), and wander in and out among the eerie formations rising from the canyon floors. Travelers may enter the park by one of three entrances but must leave their cars at established parking areas, for the average family automobile is no match for these rough pathways.

Although the park is open all year to visitors, travelers must be prepared for climatic extremes that range from temperatures of mid-90s in summer to 20° or less in winter. There are no accommodations within the park, except for simple campgrounds, but motels and resorts are just outside the park.

TORTUOUS COLORADO RIVER *cuts a twisting gorge through the park. One spectacular convolution, where it nearly crosses its own path, can best be viewed from Dead Horse Point, just outside the park boundary.*

PHILIP HYDE

CANYONLANDS NATIONAL PARK

COVERING THREE LEVELS, *the park divides into: Island in the Sky, a high mesa with an elevation of 6,000 feet, surrounded by a mezzanine (the 4,400-foot-high White Rim), which in turn overlooks the flat river valleys 500 feet below. Passenger cars can approach only to Grandview or Dead Horse Point. From Elephant Hill, the going is by foot, horse, trail bike, or jeep.*

To Moab and 163
SCENIC HIGHWAY
Mineral Bottom
Potash Mine
Ranger Station
Shafer Trail
The Neck
Upheaval Dome
ISLAND IN THE SKY
WHITE RIM
Green River Overlook
Mesa Trail
Anderson Bottom
Green
Grandview Point 6,100
Monument Basin
Junction Butte
THE MAZE
River
LAND OF STANDING ROCKS
Colorado
Candlestick Spire
Confluence Overlook
Lower Jump
Ranger Station
To Monticello and 163
Silver Stairs
Squaw Butte
Squaw Flat
North Six-Shooter Peak 6,374
GLEN CANYON RECREATION AREA
Spanish Bottom
The Grabens
CYCLONE CANYON
Devils Lane
ELEPHANT CANYON
Elephant Hill
THE NEEDLES
HORSE CANYON
Tower Ruin
South Six-Shooter Peak 6,132
CATARACT CANYON
Chesler Park
Druid Arch
Angel Arch
Upper Jump
All American Man
Big Ruin
LEGEND
Paved Roads
Unpaved Roads
4-wheel-drive Roads
Trails
Campsites
0 1 2 3 4 5
SCALE IN MILES

CRUMBLING CLIFF DWELLINGS *in Horse Canyon once sheltered Anasazi Indians, ancestors of the Pueblos.*

DAVID MUENCH

PHILIP HYDE

PREHISTORIC PICTOGRAPHS *decorate a wall in Horseshoe Canyon* (ABOVE). *Molar Rock* (BELOW) *presents a startlingly realistic form.*

DAVID MUENCH

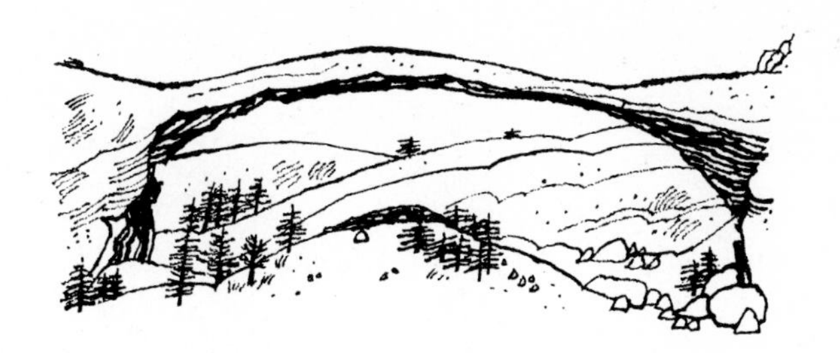

ARCHES

ROCKY CANOPIES IN CANYON COUNTRY

PARK FACTS: *Location:* Southeastern Utah. *Discovered:* early 1800s. *Established:* November 12, 1971. *Size:* 115 sq. mi. *Altitude:* 5,000 to 7,000 ft. *Climate:* Hot in summer, cold in winter. *Season:* All year. *Annual visitors:* 327,000. *Accommodations:* Campgrounds. *Activities:* Self-guiding auto tours, guided hiking trips, jeep tours (from nearby). *Information:* Supt., Arches National Park, Moab, UT 84532.

A VAST ROCK GARDEN OF SMOKY RED SANDSTONE, Arches encompasses one of the most spectacular concentrations of natural stone arches in the world. Columns and spires reach up through dancing heat waves, and streaked sworls of slickrock pour down into sandy washes dotted with wildflowers in spring. The geologic maelstrom of Salt Valley tumbles off to Klondike Bluffs, and to the east the white peaks of the La Sal Mountains range along the horizon. But impressive as they are, these formations are eclipsed by the dramatic yet delicate arcades of the arches.

The tiny grains that compose the Entrada Sandstone formation (from which most arches are eroded) were part of what, 150 million years ago, was probably a low, arid coastal plain. Eventually the sandy soil was covered by other layers and hardened into rock.

Uplifting, tilting, and erosion all combined to expose the Entrada layer to the patient forces of weathering. Water and wind cracked the sandstone, then scoured out narrow canyons separated by vertical walls or fins. Persistently, the wind and frost brushed away at the softer areas of a fin, eventually perforating it with a small window that gradually enlarged until an arch was formed.

An unofficial count indicates there are 80 to 90 arches in the park. But much of the rough, remote back country has yet to be searched systematically, and more arches may be awaiting discovery.

There are enough exploring possibilities here to suit any inclination, from an easy drive to a strenuous, day-long hike. There are several marked trails you can walk by yourself. In addition, the National Park Service conducts early morning guided walks into the confusing maze of the Fiery Furnace. Some other areas of the park can be explored by owners of four-wheel-drive vehicles.

ROCKY CANOPY *of Double Arch looms against the sky. The largest of the two openings is 163 by 157 feet. Like the other formations in the park, Double Arch was once a part of a solid layer of rock.*

ED COOPER

A GRACEFUL SPAN, *isolated in its open amphitheater, Delicate Arch is one of the park's best known features. Though the 1½-mile trail to it from Wolfe Ranch is strenuous, the reward is one of the park's most spectacular views.*

PHILIP HYDE

ED COOPER

LONGEST KNOWN NATURAL ARCH *in the world, Landscape Arch, with a span of almost 300 feet, is one of seven arches along the weaving 4-mile course of Devils Garden Trail. The 20-minute walk to this arch is relatively easy; beyond it, walking becomes more difficult.*

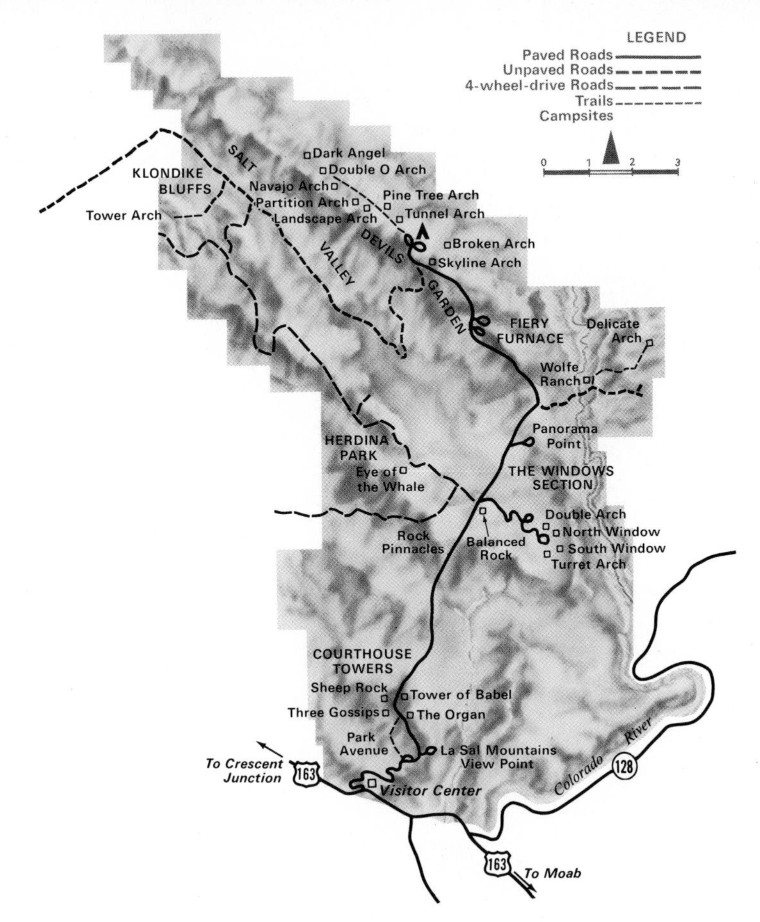

ARCHES NATIONAL PARK

SIX AREAS *in the park contain most of the scenic features. Paved roads lead to Courthouse Towers, The Windows, Fiery Furnace, and Devils Garden sections; graded roads go to Wolfe Ranch and Klondike Bluffs.*

PETRIFIED FOREST

ALCHEMY IN THE DESERT

PARK FACTS: *Location:* Eastern Arizona. *Discovered:* 1851. *Established:* National monument, 1906; national park, December 9, 1962. *Size:* 147 sq. mi. *Altitude:* 5,300 to 6,235 ft. *Climate:* Area receives less than 10 inches of moisture per year. *Season:* All year. *Annual visitors:* 958,000. *Accommodations:* None. *Activities:* Wilderness backpacking by permit. *Information:* Supt.; Petrified Forest National Park, AZ 86028.

THE FASCINATION OF PETRIFIED WOOD seems almost universal. Its attraction is more than a matter of beauty; it is partly the mystery of a magic transformation.

Mineralized wood is found in many places, but nowhere in such abundance as on the high plateau of northeastern Arizona. There, in six concentrations, great logs of jasper and agate are interspersed with smaller sections and fragments that glisten in the sun like a groundcover of gems.

Explorers reported these "stone trees" in 1851, but it was another 30 years before there were enough settlers and travelers to affect the area seriously. Then the depredations of souvenir hunters and commercial exploiters reached the point where great quantities of petrified wood were being carried off. Logs were blasted in search of the amethysts that some contained; a stamp mill was even erected nearby to crush the trees into abrasives.

The aroused citizens of Arizona, through the territorial legislature, finally won federal protection for the area, and in 1906 the Petrified Forest National Monument was established. In 1962 it was designated a national park.

Petrified wood is manufactured by nature under rather special circumstances. The mineralized logs started as living trees in a prehistoric forest. When they died and fell, they were washed down from the hills by flood waters and covered, before they could decay, with sand, mud, and volcanic ash. Eventually some geologic upheaval lifted the land, and wind and rain began to wear away the overlying sediments. After millions of years, the trees were exposed. But the wood had been replaced, cell by cell, by silica borne in the water filtering down through the overlying strata. Oxides of iron and magnesium, carried in the same water, gave the logs the red, green, and black hues we see today.

TREES THAT FELL *200 million years ago are preserved by silica, to the delight of scientists, and dyed beautifully by iron oxide and magnesium, to the fascination of all.*

DAVID MUENCH

INDIANS KNEW THIS AREA *long before the advent of white explorers. Their notes on Newspaper Rock can't be read today, but these petroglyphs may have had religious significance, been clan symbols, or simply have been "doodles."*

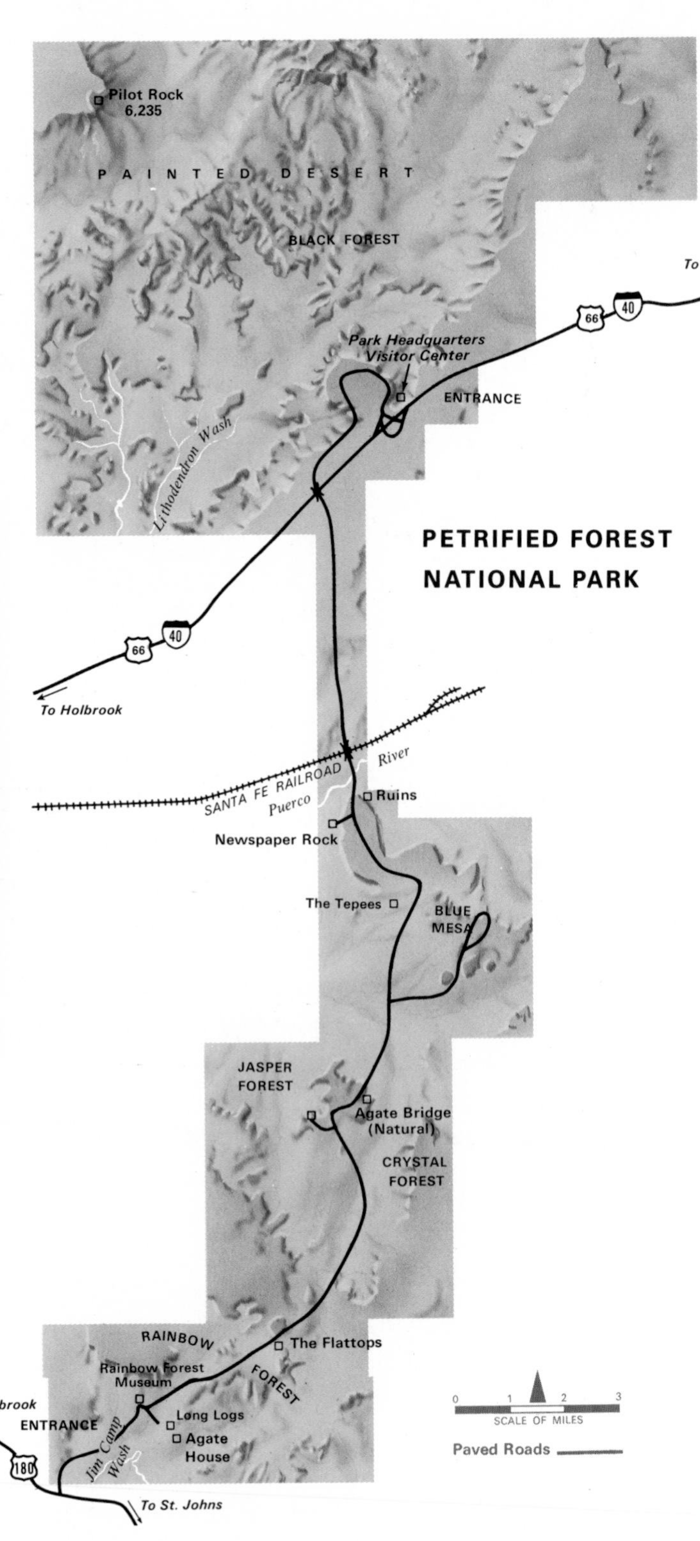

SIX SEPARATE CONCENTRATIONS *of petrified wood flank the 27-mile-long road through the neck of the park. At its north end, the Painted Desert duplicates in sandstone the fiery colors of the wood.*

MESAS, BUTTES, AND BADLANDS *cover the northern end of the park. From an observation site on Kachina Point and from overlooks along Rim Drive, you look over a bewildering array of clay hills, vividly tinged in ever-changing hues of red, pink, blue, and white.*

JOSEF MUENCH

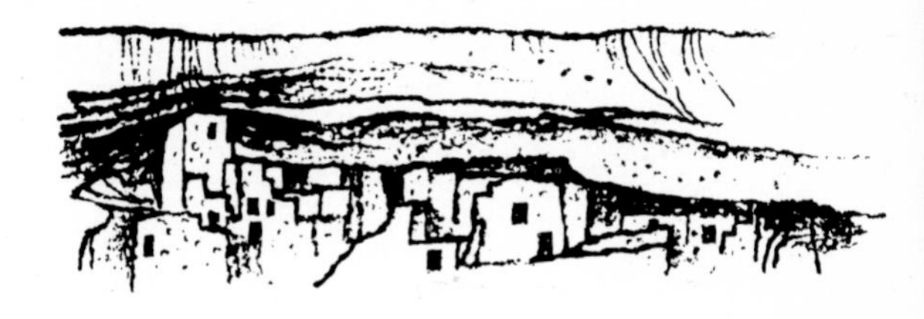

MESA VERDE

AMERICA'S OLDEST ABANDONED APARTMENTS

PARK FACTS: *Location:* Southwestern Colorado. *Discovered:* Area discovered by Spanish, 1765; Indian dwellings first discovered in 1870s. *Established:* June 29, 1906. *Size:* 81 sq. mi. Estimates indicate more than 500 dwellings within park boundaries. *Altitude:* 6,964 to 8,572 ft. *Climate:* Comfortable in summer, cold and snowy in winter. *Season:* All year. *Annual visitors:* 645,200. *Accommodations:* Campground (May through October), lodge (mid-May to mid-October). *Activities:* Guided tours through dwellings, biking (rentals), bus trips. *Information:* Supt., Mesa Verde National Park, CO 81330.

SOMETIME AFTER THE BIRTH OF CHRIST, a group of nomadic hunting people moved into the Mesa Verde and established an advanced culture which prospered until around A. D. 1300. These people became sedentary farmers, growing crops of corn, beans, and squash. They learned to weave with such consummate skill that they are often referred to as the Basket Makers.

The early people of the Mesa Verde used caves for sleeping and shelter. Their first structures were mostly pit houses—dwellings dug into the ground, then covered by logs and mud plaster. By A. D. 750, they began building houses above ground, using a pole-and-mud construction and arranging the rooms in crescent-shaped rows. This was the beginning of the pueblo period, and pottery replaced the baskets for utility purposes.

Later stone masonry techniques brought about the elaborate architecture of the cliff dwellings themselves. These sturdy, compact, apartment-like buildings stood as high as three or four stories, and sometimes contained more than 50 rooms. Often the rooms were built around courtyards that contained several kivas—underground religious chambers used for ceremonies. Complex ventilation systems in the kivas enabled the people to use fire in their rites without choking on the smoke.

Life was harsh and demanding. An average person lived only 32 to 34 years. Women and children assisted in the daily work, gathering water from nearby springs, grinding corn, repairing plastered walls, or helping in the fields. Elaborate trade networks brought in turquoise, shells from as far away as the coast of California, cotton for textile weaving, and other products.

CLIFF PALACE, *more than 700 years after its abandonment, remains the most impressive monument to the skills of its builders, who continually added to it during 100 years of occupation.*

JOSEF MUENCH

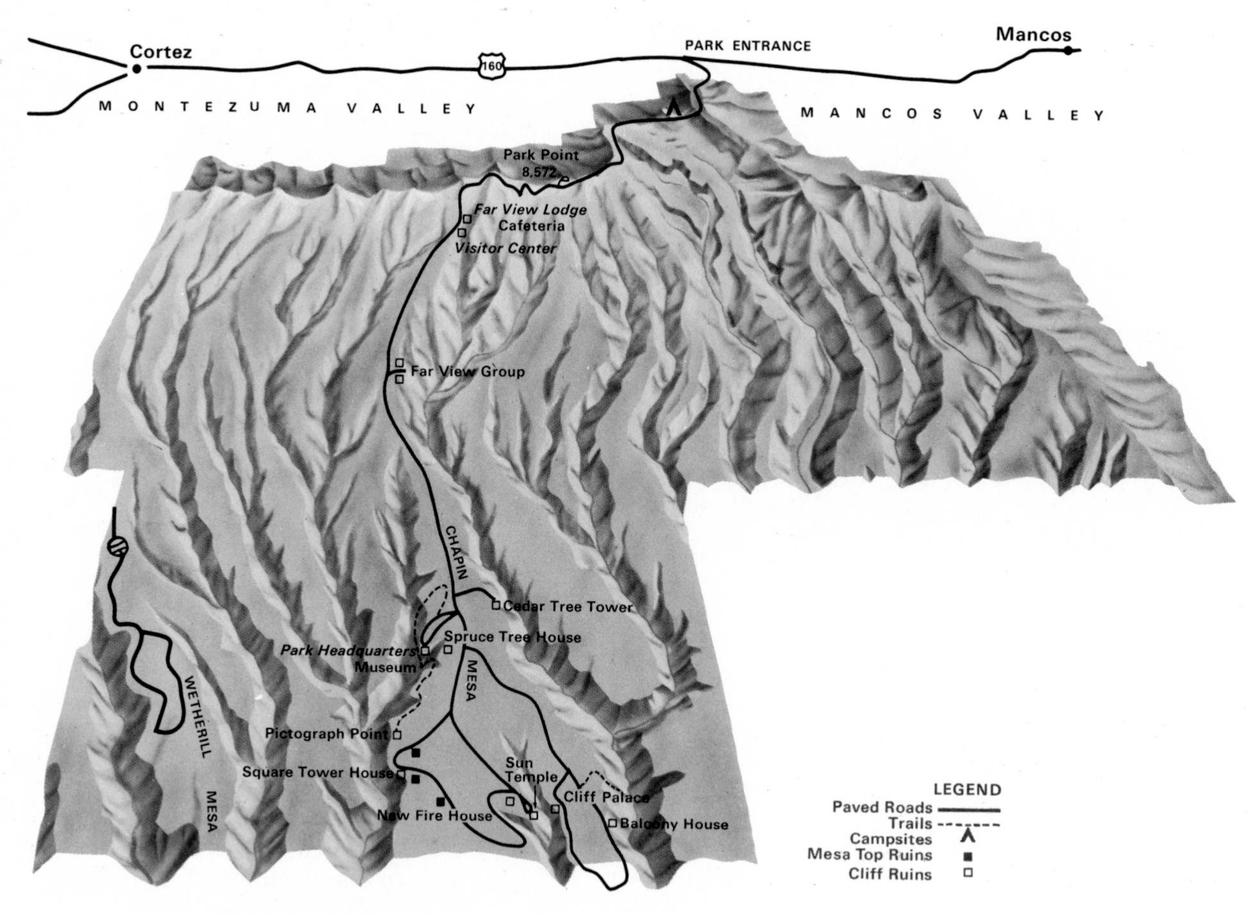

ROADS LEAD VISITORS *on a tour through time from the early pit houses of* A.D. *550 and successive eras to the peak period of the cliff dwellings in the 10th to 12th centuries.*

PIT HOUSES *were the first attempts at construction by the Mesa Verdes. The rude huts covered storage pits and apparently inspired the later ceremonial room called the kiva. The sites were eventually covered by the cliff dwellings.*

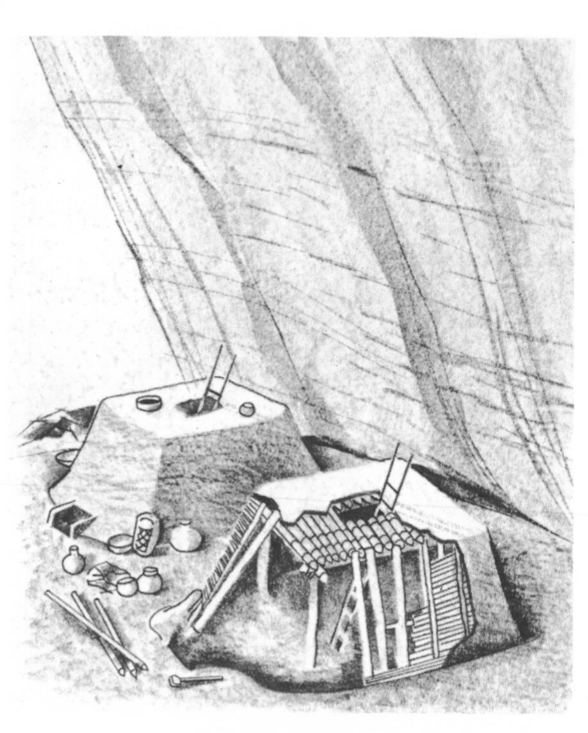

PIT HOUSES

JOSEF MUENCH

MYSTERIOUS SUN TEMPLE *sits atop the mesa. It was built long after the Mesa Verde Indians had retreated to cliff caves, and its purpose was probably religious. The building is a maze of rooms and corridors. Archeologists think many families shared in its construction.*

Then, in the late 1300s, the people began to leave Mesa Verde. An extended drought took its toll. But that was only one of the possible causes for their departure. Overuse of the land, depletion of the trees and shrubs, and over-hunting of the game animals all contributed to their difficulties. Perhaps even the social system itself began to break down. Whatever the problems were, the results were permanent, and the area was abandoned by A. D. 1300.

The uninhabited ruins endure in Mesa Verde National Park. From May 15 to October 15, ranger archeologists conduct tours of some of the outstanding ruins. During the remainder of the year, visitors can look down into the great villages and the small ones from vantage points along the roads on the mesa top. A great many artifacts were discovered by members of the ranching Wetherill family in 1888 and before the area became a park in 1906. A representative collection is in the fine park museum.

Hiking is not encouraged in Mesa Verde; there are only a few short trails. A campground located about 4 miles inside the park operates from May 1 to about October 31.

RICHARD ROWAN

IN THE HUGE, MULTIFAMILY DWELLINGS, *families added rooms as need arose, spreading laterally until they ran out of space, then adding second, third, and fourth stories to original apartments. Tiny rooms were for storage and sleeping. Daily activity went on in open courts, on kiva or apartment roofs.*

RICHARD ROWAN

FOR ONE GIDDY MOMENT, *contemporary visitors to the cliff dwellings can experience life as the original inhabitants lived it. They must climb a long ladder into Balcony House. Well sheltered in its cliffside cave, Spruce Tree House* (BELOW) *is one of the best preserved of the dwellings. It contains 114 rooms.*

ED COOPER

CARLSBAD CAVERNS

FANTASY BENEATH THE DESERT

PARK FACTS: *Location:* Southeastern New Mexico. *Discovered:* Settlers knew of caves in 1880s. *Established:* National monument, 1923; national park, May 14, 1930. *Size:* 73 sq. mi. Explored caverns cover 20 mi.; 3 mi. open to public. *Altitude:* 4,400 ft. at surface. *Climate:* Surface temperatures 0°F/-18°C to 100°F/38°C; caverns remain at constant 56°F/13°C. *Season:* All year. *Annual visitors:* 867,300. *Accommodations:* None. *Activities:* Underground interpretive trips, primitive lantern trips into New Cave on limited basis, guided nature walks, backpacking. *Information:* Supt., Carlsbad Caverns National Park, 3225 National Parks Highway, Carlsbad, NM 88220.

AN INFINITY IN TIME AND THE INFINITE POWER of trickling water have hollowed scores of caverns out of the limestone beneath the southeast corner of New Mexico. During the latter part of the 60 million years this has been going on, oozing drops have left mineral trails behind them in the myriad rock sculptures that give the Carlsbad Caverns, the largest of all these caves, their eerie charm.

Nobody knows how extensive these caverns are. More than 20 miles have been explored, at depths ranging down to 1,024 feet below the surface. As many as 5 million bats have shared one mile of cavern. At present, only three of the most amazing miles are open to park visitors.

The easily walked tour trail passes through great vaults with names like Green Lake Room, King's Palace, and Queen's Chamber, where the rock formations support even more picturesque names: Iceberg, Bone Yard, Totem Pole, and the Rock of Ages are examples. The biggest of these chambers (the Big Room) is 2,000 feet long and 200 feet from floor to soaring ceiling. The walls are hung with rock draperies. (The stalagmites grow from the floor up, the stalactites from the ceiling down.)

The full tour starts at the natural entrance to the cave and gives visitors a fine look at the caverns as the trail winds along the floor then high along a comfortingly wide ledge on one wall. Improbable as it may seem, a box luncheon is served at a restaurant located halfway along the trail, 750 feet below the surface. A shortened tour starts with the elevator ride down to the central area of the caverns, where it joins the other tour for a stroll around the Big Room. Everyone returns to the visitor center on the surface by elevator.

BEAUTIFUL HUES *in the formations can be explained in scientific terms. The rock is calcite or aragonite—crystalline forms of limestone—colored by iron oxide or other minerals. But their rich luster when they are wet defies chemical analysis.*

JOSEF MUENCH

The caverns are 56° the year around, whether the desert above is enduring the 0° winds of winter or the 100° heat of summer.

There is a surface side to the park, which supports a busy desert life community. Most of it is nocturnal, and the star attraction is the evening bat flight. The bat caves themselves are not open to touring; although bats are quite clean, their quarters are not. The best views of this striking spectacle are near the cavern mouth, where a ranger naturalist gives a short explanation of what is about to happen, just before the swirling storm erupts, within a few minutes of sundown. The greatest flights are in summer, when the whole colony is in residence and actively pursuing night-flying insects. A great number of the bats migrate south for the winter; in the coldest season the remaining ones go into a state of suspended animation, and the flights dwindle to nothing.

The park also has an abundance of small mammals, desert reptiles, and birds living in its scrub vegetation. Careful observation will reveal ground squirrels, skunks, raccoons, ringtails, foxes, many types of lizards, turkey vultures, and an occasional golden eagle.

The presence of the caverns has been known for a thousand years. Some wandering Indians used the cavern mouth for shelter but they did not test the temper of any god of the underworld by penetrating far inside. That was left to the turn-of-the-century bat guano miners. One of them, a young resident of the area, named James Larkin White, found himself drawn to serious explorations. His interest grew to passion, and his passion led to the establishment of the caverns as a national monument in 1923 and a national park in 1930. White's reward was a term as chief ranger of the park he helped establish.

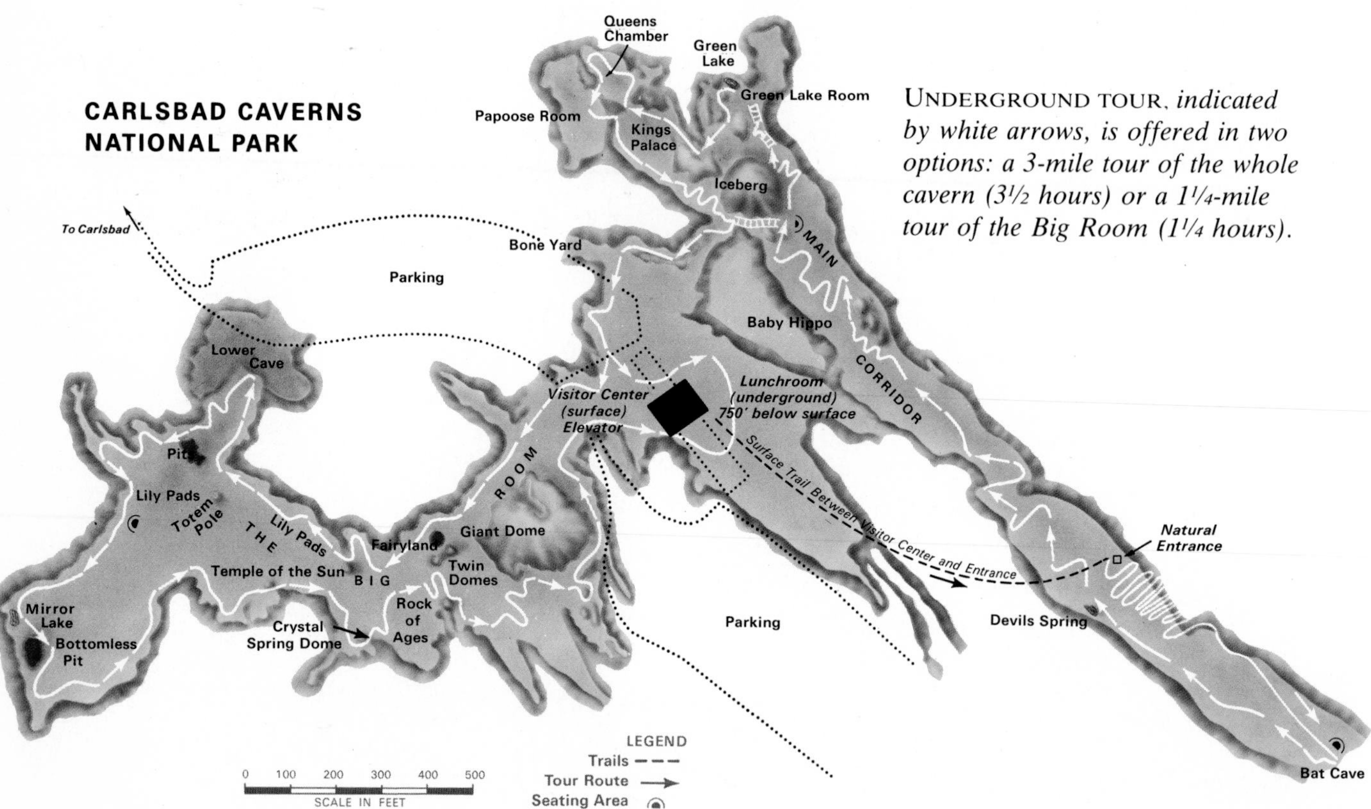

UNDERGROUND TOUR, *indicated by white arrows, is offered in two options: a 3-mile tour of the whole cavern (3½ hours) or a 1¼-mile tour of the Big Room (1¼ hours).*

ED COOPER

THE GIANT DOME (LEFT) *bulks massively in the Big Room. Rising to 62 feet above the floor of the cavern, the column approaches 20 feet in diameter. China Wall* (BELOW) *casts its shadow on the floor of New Cave. This cave was discovered in 1937 by a goat herder looking for lost animals.*

ED COOPER

HOW THE CAVERNS WERE FORMED

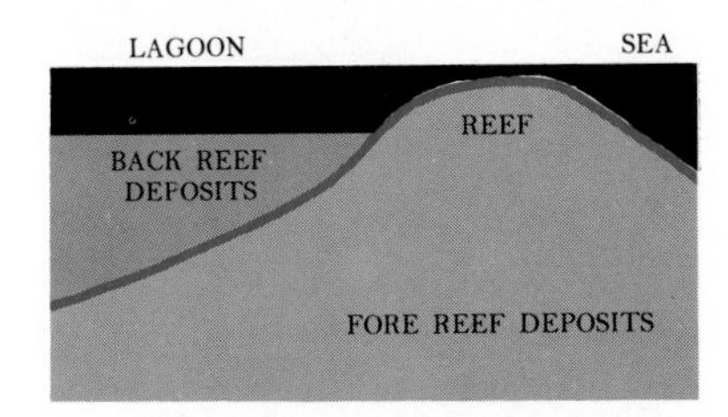

ABOUT 200 MILLION YEARS AGO, *the dome of the cavern formation was a reef in a Permian sea. The sea deposited sediments in the lagoon, then rose and covered the whole reef with deep deposits. Two succeeding uplifts of the earth's crust raised the formation above the water table. Fractures in the limestone allowed seepage that formed the caverns; then seepage of ground water from rain and snow fashioned rock sculptures.*

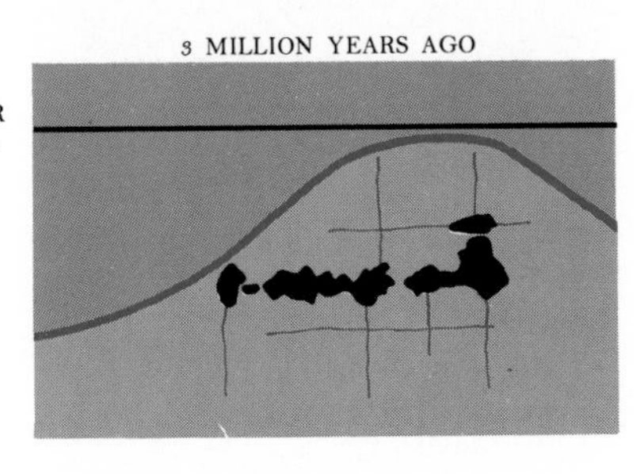

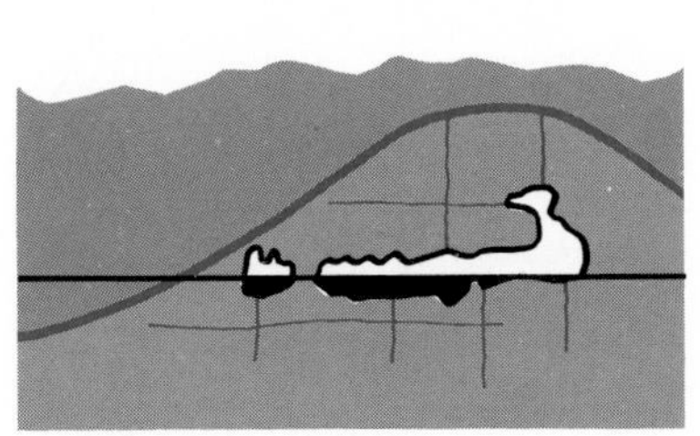

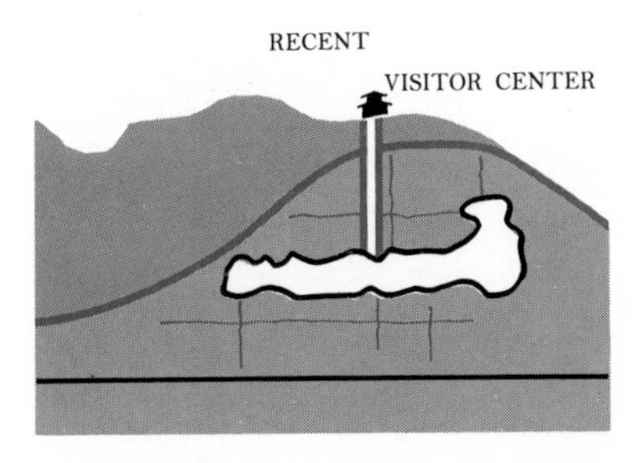

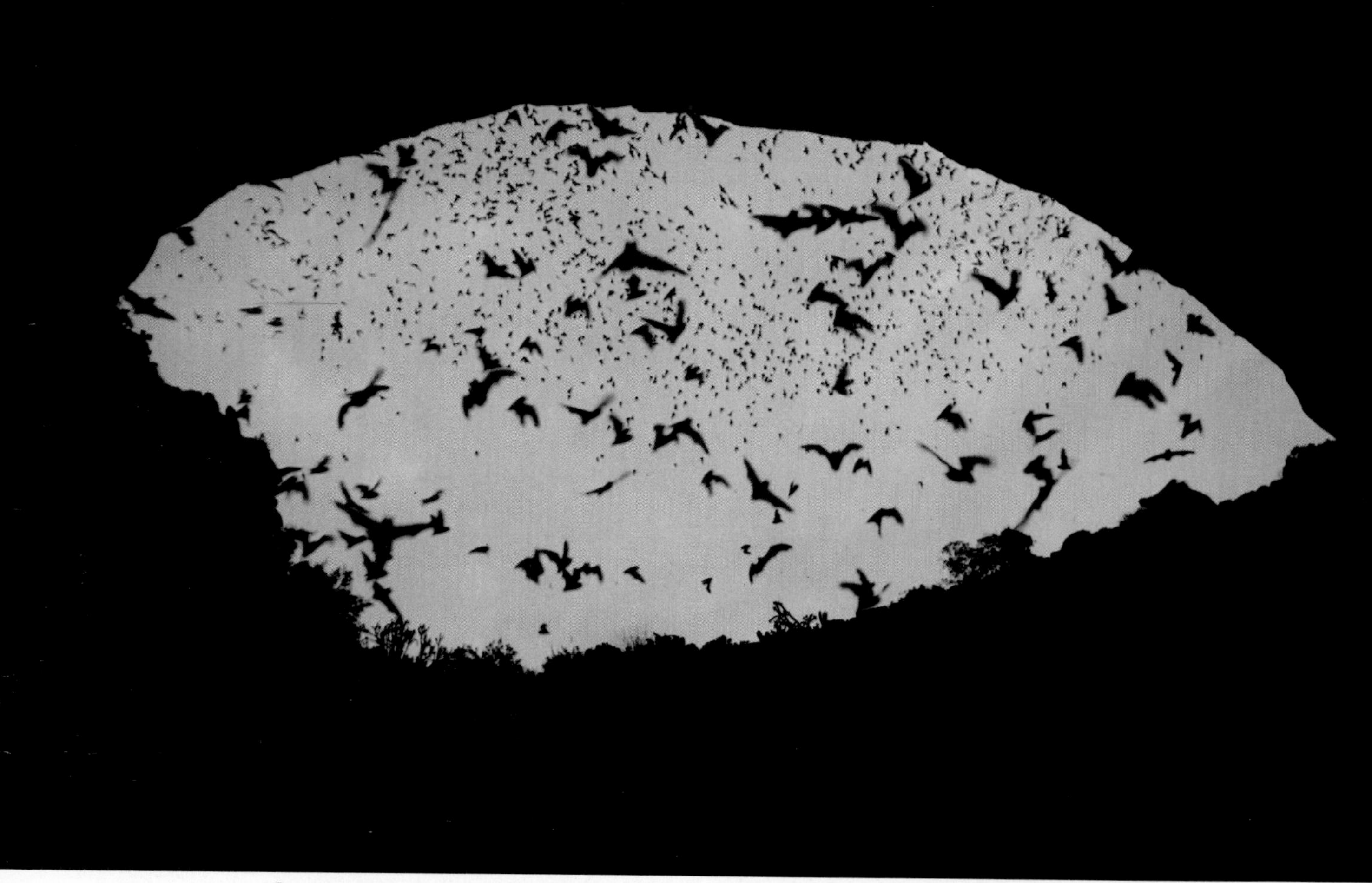

IN THE SPAN OF HALF AN HOUR *each evening at sunset, up to 5,000 bats per minute fly from the main cavern. They fan out over a 50-mile radius to catch and eat several tons of winged insects before dawn, when they return to the cavern to sleep the day away, hanging head down in dense clusters.* RONAL C. KERBO

THE REMARKABLE SONAR OF BATS

A BAT CAN NAB A MOSQUITO *on the wing, dodge a wind-whipped tree limb, and wing merrily on his way through the blackest night of the year. How? The bats that live in these caves are in effect FM transmitters. They emit a high-frequency note which exceeds by many times the range of a human voice, yet lasts a thousandth of a second or less. They hear the minute portion of their sound that is reflected by prey—or an obstacle—and "lock in" with ever-faster beeps until they nab the food or dodge the obstacle with a daring bit of aerobatics. Scientists find it very difficult to jam the emissions, but impaired hearing or muting renders a bat nearly helpless in flight.*

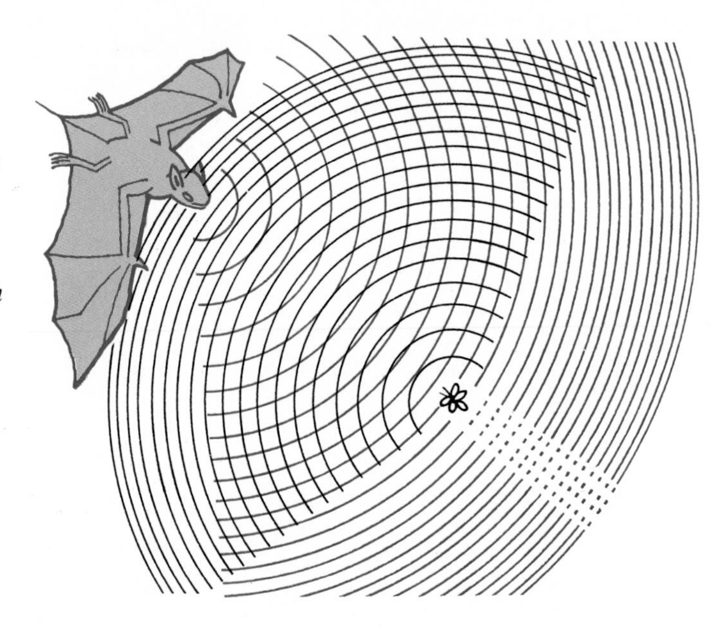

RONAL C. KERBO

RONAL C. KERBO

OUTSIDE THE CAVERNS *the desert holds other fascinations. Wildlife abounds, and spring brings wildflowers and blooming cactus.* ABOVE LEFT: *A young ringtail snoozes during the day; at night, he'll prowl the park on a hunt for small rodents.* ABOVE RIGHT: *A brilliant claret cup cactus and a wild daisy enliven the scene.*

RONAL C. KERBO

INCREDIBLE RED SKY *that often follows a desert sunset strikingly emphasizes the dramatic silhouette of a torrey yucca.*

ROCKY MOUNTAIN

ASTRIDE THE CONTINENTAL DIVIDE

PARK FACTS: *Location:* North central Colorado. *Discovered:* 1859. *Established:* January 26, 1915. *Size:* 412 sq. mi. *Altitude:* 7,620 to 14,256 ft. *Climate:* Cool, pleasant; perpetual snows mantle highest summits and valley walls. *Season:* All year, but main cross-park highway, Trail Ridge Road, closed mid-October to late May. *Annual visitors:* 3,038,000. *Accommodations:* Campgrounds (Longs Peak restricted to tent camping). *Activities:* Hiking, backpacking, fishing, horseback riding, mountaineering, cross-country skiing, downhill skiing (Hidden Valley). *Information:* Supt., Rocky Mountain NP, Estes Park, CO 80517.

THIS IS THE HIGH COUNTRY. The skyline is saw-toothed with jutting granite, unsoftened by vegetation, for tree line is at 11,500 feet. From one spot you can count 72 peaks that rise above that height. Eighteen are more than 13,000 feet. Snow patches remain on the crags the year around in protected spots, and high cirques preserve the remnants of glaciers.

Rocky Mountain National Park has been called a primer of glacial geology. Even the most casual observer must notice the great rock amphitheaters where the glaciers formed, the U-shaped valleys carved when the ice began to move, the moraines where the loose rocks collected. Only a few small glaciers are found here now, but the marks left by ice are all around.

Guardian of all is lofty Longs Peak, whose summit rises to 14,256 feet. It dominates the front range and can be seen from far out on the plains to the east. The park takes in about 412 square miles of the most scenic part of north central Colorado. Below the towering peaks is a high vacationland of quiet lakes and plunging streams, grassy meadows and rugged gorges. One of the remarkable aspects of the park is its widespread alpine tundra, that dense carpet of miniature plants that thrives in cold climates.

The park shelters countless wild creatures. You may see mule deer, herds of elk, industrious beavers—and, if you're lucky, bighorn sheep, the symbol of the park.

Despite the rugged terrain, the park is easily accessible. Much of its splendor can be viewed at a distance from main roads. The most famous, Trail Ridge Road, reaches an altitude of 12,183 feet and stays above timberline for 11 miles.

"ABOVE TIMBERLINE" *is a phrase that takes on real meaning in Rocky Mountain National Park. At Rock Cut, nearly 12,000 feet in elevation and almost 600 feet above the tree line, densely wooded Forest Canyon is far below.*

DARWIN VAN CAMPEN

To enjoy this park to the fullest, to experience both its grandeur and its quiet peace, you must penetrate it by trail. Such exquisite spots as Loch Vale, Jewel, Fern, and Odessa lakes are reached only by those willing to walk or ride on horseback. More than 300 miles of trails lead to such rewarding destinations.

The park is open all year. Spring is shy and waits until late April or early May to display its finery. The long days of summer, when the sun is warm and the lakes and sky rich blue, are followed by the spectacular advent of the Colorado autumn. The mountain foliage blazes scarlet and gold, the days grow crisp, and through the clear air you may hear the trumpeted challenge of the big bull elk as he gathers his harem. Then the snows come again, a white blanket settles over the Rockies, and the skiers and snowshoers come back into their own.

Those who today enjoy the bounties of this mountain playground can thank one man for preserving it for their pleasure. Enos Mills, writer and naturalist, sometimes called the "John Muir of the Rockies," campaigned for the park for years against strong opposition. When at length it was established in 1915, its creation was universally credited to the persistence of Mills and his followers.

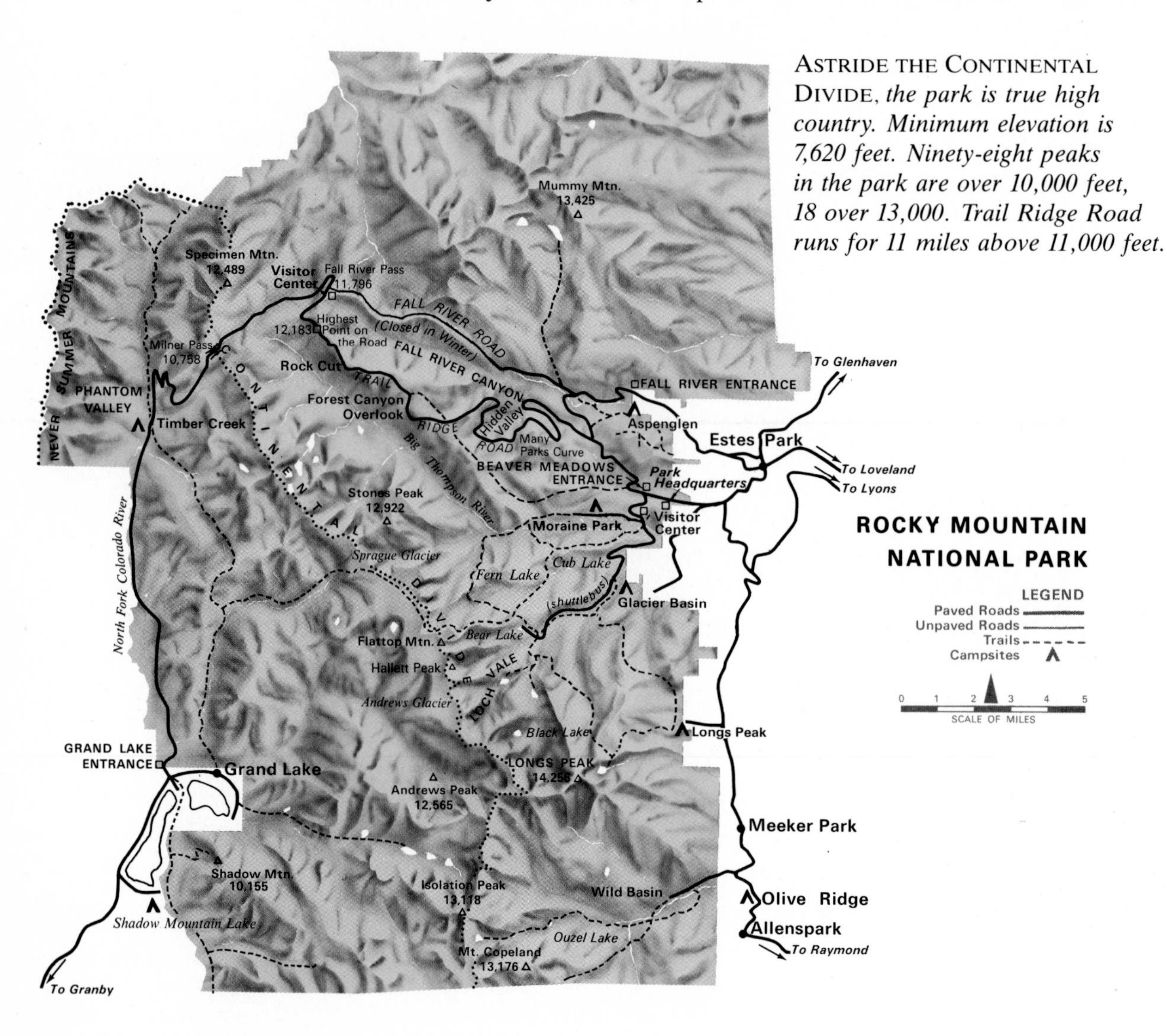

ASTRIDE THE CONTINENTAL DIVIDE, *the park is true high country. Minimum elevation is 7,620 feet. Ninety-eight peaks in the park are over 10,000 feet, 18 over 13,000. Trail Ridge Road runs for 11 miles above 11,000 feet.*

DAVID MUENCH

DUCKY KNOWLTON

NEVER SUMMER MOUNTAINS *come into view west of Milner Pass on Trail Ridge Road. The Rockies in this area are composed of a mixture of hard granites and gneisses.* LEFT: *only a day old, this trusting baby elk will soon run with the herd. Nearly extinguished by hunters before the park was established, the elk (wapiti) are a common sight now.*

ENJOYING THE TRANQUILITY, *two young hikers rest beside lily-strewn Cub Lake. More than 300 miles of park trails range from easy strolls to overnight trips into remote back country.*

DOROTHY KRELL

FIND THE CLIMBERS! *There are five clinging to "The Diamond," one of several technical climbing routes on the east face of Longs Peak. The photograph was taken from Chasm View. A route up the north face starts out from here.*

ED COOPER

A FLOWER-RICH MEADOWLAND *grows above the tree line. The alpine tundra of this park is the best example of this type of vegetation preserved in the National Park System. Alpine tundra is found on mountains above tree line; arctic tundra occurs beyond the limit of trees in the far north or south.* DAVID MUENCH

ROLF ZILLMER

TO LEARN ABOUT THE PARK, *attentive group has joined a ranger-led hike from Moraine Park Visitor Center on Bear Lake Road.* (RIGHT) *Alpine tundra is the fascination near Alpine Visitors Center on Trail Ridge Road. If you look closely, you'll find a wealth of fragile blooms to photograph, or simply admire. But walk carefully—it has taken many, many years for some of these plants to reach their present tiny size.*

DOROTHY KRELL

GRAND TETON

RENDEZVOUS FOR MOUNTAINEERS

PARK FACTS: *Location:* West central Wyoming. *Discovered:* 1807. *Established:* February 26, 1929; Jackson Hole added September 14, 1950. *Size:* 485 sq. mi. *Altitude:* 6,400 to 13,770 ft. *Climate:* Warm, dry summers with cool nights, occasional storms. Winter snows average 120 inches. *Season:* All year. *Annual visitors:* 4,160,000. *Accommodations:* Campgrounds, cabins, trailer village, climber's ranch, guest ranch, lodge. *Activities:* Hiking, boating, biking, Snake River float trips, lake cruises, fishing, swimming (String, Leigh, Jackson lakes and lodge), backpacking, mountaineering, guided horse trips, bus tours, cross-country skiing, ice fishing. *Information:* Supt., Grand Teton NP, Moose, WY 83012.

THE TETONS RISE FROM THE COUNTRYSIDE around them like a craggy island from the sea. Few American landscapes are more dramatic, more awe-inspiring, or more beautiful than these mountains of northwest Wyoming. From 100 or even 50 miles away, they seem little more than wisps of cloud. As you draw closer they begin to assume more substantial form, then suddenly their full impact strikes you, as if they had exploded from the level floor of Jackson Hole. Many ranges are more extensive and many mountains are higher, gradually ascending with foothills as steppingstones. But there is nothing gradual about the Tetons in their sheer, 7,000-foot rise from the level plain.

Grand Teton National Park contains a little less than 500 square miles. It is smaller than many parks, but within it is packed more scenery, more history, more animals, more boating and fishing, more hiking and mountain climbing than in many areas twice its size.

The scenic grandeur of the Tetons is that of the Sierra Nevada or of the Rockies telescoped into a range less than 40 miles long. The majesty of the Grand Teton, with its 13,770-foot summit and its companion peaks, Mount Owen, and South and Middle Tetons, reflected in the placid waters of Jenny Lake, is almost overwhelming. Glaciers nestle in the cirques, streams tumble and cascade from high places, mountain lakes reflect the blue of a Wyoming sky, and in the valley below, the Snake River winds its way to Jackson Lake and on eventually to the Columbia.

Two hundred miles of trails beckon the hiker and horseman—trails that lead to lakes buried in virgin wilderness, through deep canyons, over high passes above timberline, and to mountaintops. There are trails for every mood and

GOLDEN ASPEN *frame a view of incomparable Grand Teton. In view from nearly every part of the park, "the Grand" and its rugged neighbors never fail to catch and hold the eye.*

RUSSELL LAMB

every temperament, from short, level walks to long, strenuous hikes. The Tetons have long been the objective of serious climbers from this country and Europe—and few American peaks are more respected. Those who know are reluctant to rank the Alps above the Tetons in difficulty of ascent. It is little wonder that the last two peaks in this range were not conquered until 1930. Such climbs are not for the novice; for those who respond to the challenge, a mountaineering school operates here.

The history of the area has a fascination all its own. Probably the first white man to penetrate it was John Colter of the Lewis and Clark expedition in 1807. He was followed by the Astorians, who crossed Teton Pass in 1811. French-Canadian trappers in 1819 saw the three peaks from the west and referred to them as *Les Trois Tetons* (The Three Breasts).

From 1824 on, the area was a center of fur trade activity. Mountain men, among them Jim Bridger, William Sublette, Thomas Fitzpatrick, Jedediah Smith, Joseph Meek, knew the country well. One of the largest of the fur rendezvous, that of 1832, was held in Pierre's Hole across the range to the west. Still later in the 80s, it was cattle country; the town of Jackson yet retains a certain flavor of the days before tourists replaced steers in importance. Fictional characters, too, have furthered Jackson's fame. Here it was that the Virginian said, "When you call me that, *smile*," and it was to Honeymoon Island on Leigh Lake that he brought his bride. Owen Wister's book did much to publicize the romance of the Tetons.

As early as 1920, Jackson Hole was becoming known for its versions of the dude ranch, an institution that has grown in popularity over the years. Through it many an Easterner has fallen in love with the freedom and informality of Western life. It is here, for the first time, that many a tenderfoot has used a Western saddle and worn Western clothes; experienced the odors of sagebrush flats, pine forests, and a campfire; found luxury in falling asleep under the stars, and pleasure in the wash of windlashed rain in his face during a mountain storm.

Jackson Hole contains one of the largest remaining elk herds. Herds of 7,000 to 9,000 wintering on the National Elk Refuge north of Jackson, adjacent to the park, are a major attraction.

No road penetrates the mountainous west side of this park, but on the east, good highways traverse it in a general north-south direction. One skirts the east shore of Jackson and Jenny lakes at the very foot of the peaks reflected in their waters. The Jackson Hole Highway, a few miles to the east, follows the Snake River and affords a better opportunity to view the range as a whole.

The season of greatest activity is from early June through Labor Day, although the highway from Jackson through the park and over Togwotee Pass to the east is kept open throughout the winter. The park is approached from all four directions by highway.

THE MAGIC OF THE GRAND TETONS *has enthralled viewers ever since the range was first discovered. Indians, fur traders, cattlemen, and tourists have in succession felt the spell of this dramatic country. The symmetrical mountains take on varying coloration, ranging from gray to blue to purple, and sometimes a subtle blend of the colors in a cloud-filled sky.*

DAVID MUENCH

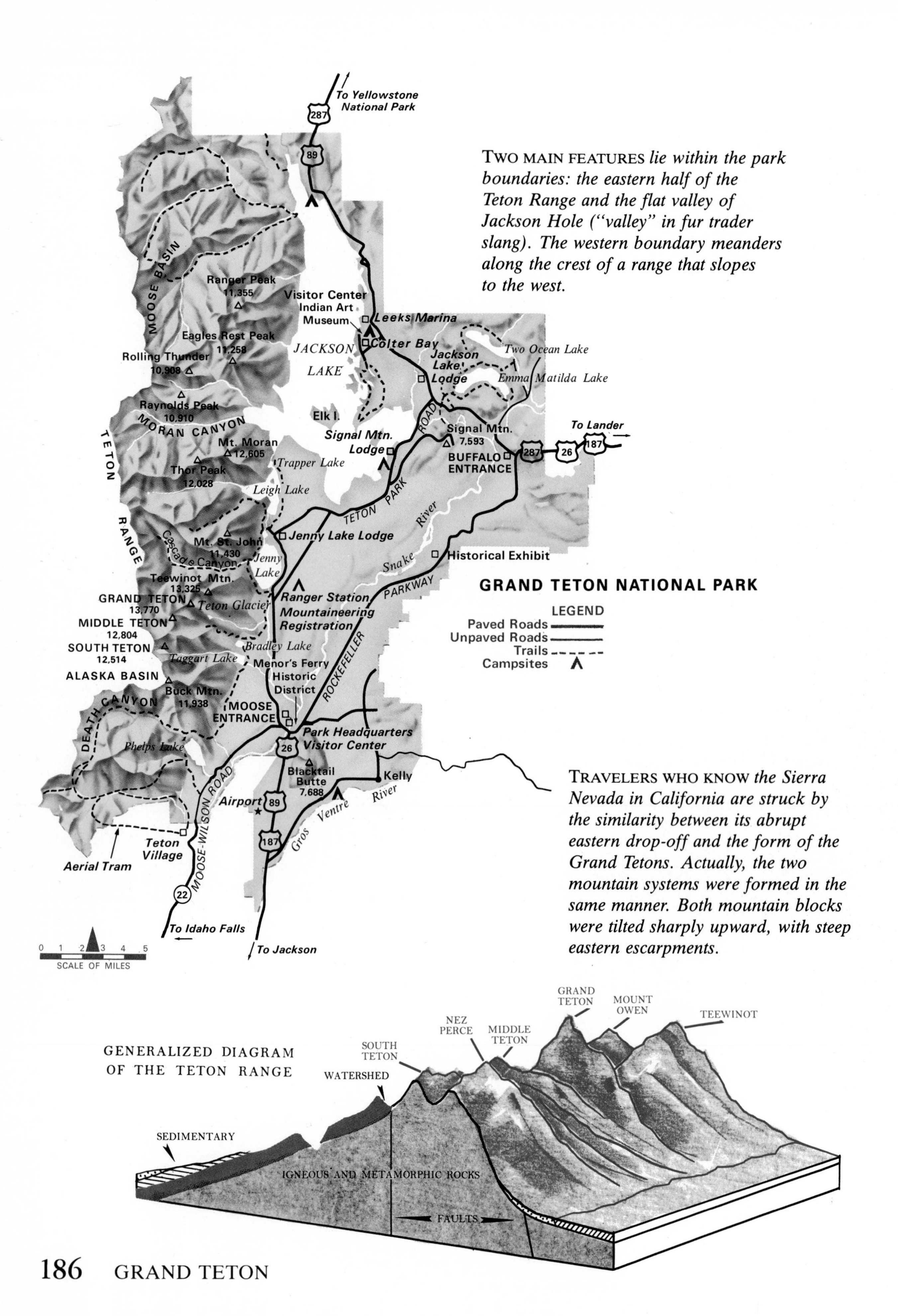

TWO MAIN FEATURES *lie within the park boundaries: the eastern half of the Teton Range and the flat valley of Jackson Hole ("valley" in fur trader slang). The western boundary meanders along the crest of a range that slopes to the west.*

TRAVELERS WHO KNOW *the Sierra Nevada in California are struck by the similarity between its abrupt eastern drop-off and the form of the Grand Tetons. Actually, the two mountain systems were formed in the same manner. Both mountain blocks were tilted sharply upward, with steep eastern escarpments.*

DOROTHY KRELL

"MOUNTAINS WITHOUT FOOTHILLS," *the peaks rise straight from the level valley floor. Seen from a distance, they seem mere clouds on the horizon, then suddenly the impact of their sheer, 7,000-foot rise becomes apparent and awe-inspiring.*

LAZING DOWN THE SNAKE, *rafters have time to enjoy splendid views of the Tetons and a landscape little changed since the days when mountain men trapped here. It's not unusual to pass elk, moose, or deer drinking at the water's edge, or to see hawks, herons, and sometimes even a rare osprey or an eagle.*

DOROTHY KRELL

IN WINTER DRESS, *the winding Snake River and the snow-frosted Tetons are a Christmas card scene. In the 1870s, settlers here were nearly wiped out by blizzards; today mountain slopes at Jackson, just outside the park, ring with the exuberant cries of skiers enjoying a more tamed winter scene. Ski touring is becoming a popular winter sport in the park.*

RUSSELL LAMB

DOMINATING THE VIEW *across Jackson Lake, massive, glacier-draped Mount Moran reflects in the calm water. The man-made lake occupies a large share of the park. A boat trip at sunset offers beautiful views of the mountain's ever-changing colors.*

RUSSELL LAMB

ED COOPER

A MAGNET FOR MOUNTAINEERS, *the jagged spires of the Tetons attract climbers from all over the world. First attempts in the 1870s to scale the Grand Teton failed, but by now several thousand mountaineers have entered their names in the log on the summit.* ABOVE: *Grand Teton viewed from the top of Middle Teton.*

CLIMBING MAP OF THE GRAND TETON, NORTH FACE

X—Rappel points
Y—Finger-and-toe climbs
Z—Difficult belays

SIXTEEN ROUTES *lead to the summit of Grand Teton, ranging in difficulty from third to fifth-class climbs, in mountaineering language.*

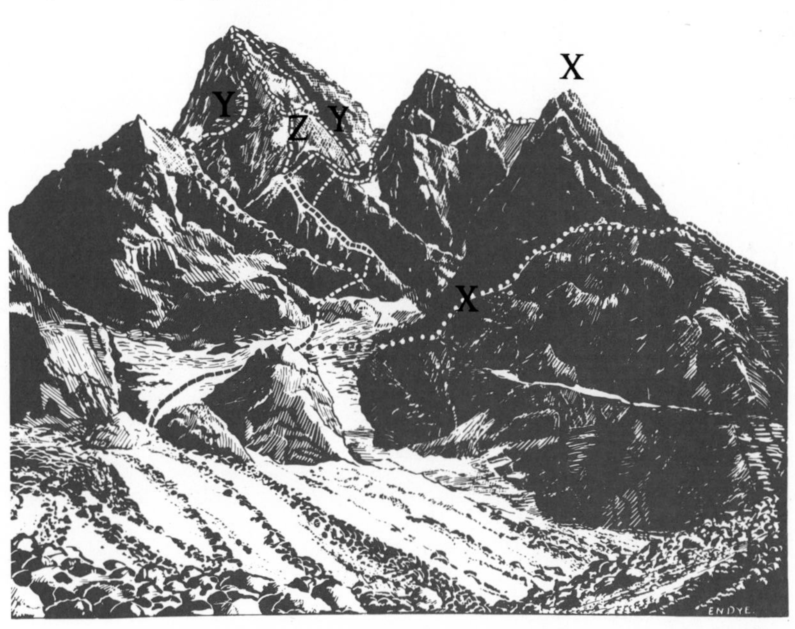

E. N. DYE, FROM SIERRA CLUB'S "CLIMBER'S GUIDE TO TETON RANGE"

DAVID MUENCH

BETTY RANDALL

A FIELD OF BALSAMROOT *brightens the view across the valley. The colorful, sunflower-like flowers come into bloom early on the sunny flatlands. As the season progresses, wildflowers bloom at higher elevations.* ABOVE: *Endangered trumpeter swans find protection in the park.*

YELLOWSTONE

THE GRAND OLD PARK

PARK FACTS: *Location:* Northwestern Wyoming. *Discovered:* 1807. *Established:* March 1, 1872. *Size:* 3,472 sq. mi. *Altitude:* 5,314 to 11,358 ft. *Climate:* Mild summer days, cool nights. Winter temperatures from below freezing, heavy snowfall. *Season:* All year (official season May 1-Oct. 31). *Annual visitors:* 2,623,000. *Accommodations:* Campgrounds (Mammoth open all year), cabins, trailer village, hotels, lodges. *Activities:* Fishing, boating, horseback riding, stagecoach rides, boat and bus tours, hiking, backpacking, cross-country skiing, snowmobiling. *Information:* Supt., Yellowstone National Park, WY 82190.

YELLOWSTONE IS THE "TYPICAL" NATIONAL PARK of anecdote and caricature, of plentiful bears, of elbow-to-elbow fishermen and hopelessly tangled trout lines, and of incredible summer hordes of wandering tourists.

On the other side of the coin, Yellowstone works a magic spell in return for nothing but time and attention. It is not a place that jibes with personal timetables. Travelers go to Yellowstone to witness things happening more than to look at static scenery, and seldom—at any site—will nature's performance coincide with one's arrival. So the visitor moves along, trusting to luck, or settles down and waits. In good time, sunlight reaches the bottom of a golden canyon and a waterfall's spray rises through rainbows. An osprey finally alights on the pinnacle-top nest in the telephoto viewfinder. The bull moose emerges from forest shadow and wades out into a marsh. A family of playful young grizzlies comes wrestling and tumbling through a wind-rippled prairie. A brown trout—big enough to feed a whole family—takes the lure and then sounds. The Sapphire Pool belches a brief alert and then explodes into snowy jets that climb for the sky.

There is hot-spring activity of one kind or another in many countries. But nowhere is there so much of it, nowhere is it so spectacular, and nowhere has it been so considerately cared for.

Neither color illustrations nor postcards can memorialize the diverse beauty of the countless ways hot water comes out of the ground in Yellowstone: the flooding colors of spectrum and algae, the transparence of bubble-starred pools dropping away into darkness, the echoed thumping of unheralded distant geysers in the night, the smell of hydrogen sulfide, the sky-flung plumes of water.

AWESOME GORGE *of the Yellowstone River is a stunning surprise to travelers when they first encounter it. The gentle, forested countryside scarcely prepares the visitor for chasm walls glowing with reds, ochres, and yellows. The park was named for this colorful canyon.*

STEVEN FULLER

NATIONAL PARK SERVICE

SO UNBELIEVABLE WERE THE TALES *about Yellowstone told by the first explorers that two expeditions were sent to the region to determine the truth, if any, in their reports. This photograph, taken in 1871 by W. H. Jackson, shows the second fact-finding expedition, the Geological Survey's Hayden Expedition. Reports of this party plus Jackson's photographs helped convince Congress that Yellowstone country should be made a national park.*

ALTHOUGH THE WONDERS OF YELLOWSTONE were discovered in 1807 and rumors about them circulated for decades, they were laughed off as tall tales, too fantastic to believe, until nearly 1870.

Actual discovery is credited to a member of the Lewis and Clark expedition named John Colter, who left the group to explore and trap on his own. By 1837, the story of his adventures was widely enough known to have reached novelist Washington Irving, who wrote about Colter's description of an area east of Yellowstone, which cited its "gloomy terrors, hidden fires, smoking pits, noxious streams, and the all-pervading smell of brimstone." That area became known among trappers as "Colter's Hell," a name that was later applied to Yellowstone.

Trappers wandered throughout Yellowstone for 60 years after Colter's visit, and tales about its marvels were common among them. However, little of the information reached the general public. The mountain men were a close-knit and unlettered fraternity. They were known as braggarts and liars, and their stories were accepted as typical frontier "roarbacks."

But as settlement advanced in the territories nearby, prominent citizens began to take an interest in checking into these preposterous tales. In 1869, a party of three men spent more than a month exploring the eastern geyser basins and reported their findings to a still skeptical public. Their observations, however, spurred a more famous group to follow the trail to Yellowstone. This was the Washburn-Langford-Doane expedition, whose exploits led to the founding of the National Park Service, as described in the opening chapter.

This party of nineteen men, full of exuberance and wonder, systematically explored the area, keeping careful records as they progressed. They named the thermal features—favoring the Devil and all his works—but by common agreement, they refrained from naming anything for themselves. (Their names were later bestowed on some of the peaks and rivers.) After completing their survey, they met at a famous campfire at the intersection of the Gibbon, Firehole, and Madison rivers and there reached the historic decision to work for legislation to protect the wonderland from exploitation.

After returning home, they lectured, published articles in magazines and newspapers, and campaigned to have the area set aside as a public preserve. As an early result of their pressures, United States Geologist F. V. Hayden led a scientific expedition to Yellowstone to authenticate their findings. His enthusiastic endorsement of their observations, coupled with a superb set of photographs by W. H. Jackson, helped to speed the enactment of the historic legislation that created the first national park in the world in 1872.

FROM FREEMAN TILDEN'S "FOLLOWING THE FRONTIER"

CARRYING UMBRELLAS AS BADGES OF LEADERSHIP, *Indian chiefs line up to receive President Chester A. Arthur in 1883. The presidential party traveled 350 miles on horseback to visit the park, catch fish, shoot buffalo, and powwow with the Indians en route.*

PERCHED ON BRITTLE FORMATIONS *of Minerva Terrace, a touring party of women and children strike a formal pose for photographer Frank J. Haynes in 1888.*

Unfortunately, farsighted as the legislators were for their day, they did not provide for all eventualities in the new law nor did they appropriate funds, and the park administration struggled for years sorely handicapped.

The park was located miles from nowhere and in the midst of territory still plagued by unfriendly Indians. Just four years after creation of the park, General Custer suffered his last stand a scant 130 miles away. In 1877, the Nez Perce in the closing days of their bloody 1,600-mile retreat from Oregon, captured a party of tourists camped on Firehole River and killed two from another party. A few days later, the warriors were defeated in their final battle north of the park. When, two years later, the park superintendent's headquarters was erected, it was equipped with a gun turret on the roof.

Even after the Indians were quieted, tourists faced an arduous trek to reach the park. In 1878, they had a choice of two routes: a northern one from Bismarck that was 1,052 miles long—820 miles by steamboat and 232 by stagecoach—and took 12 to 14 days. The southern access from Ogden required 1,183 miles of train travel followed by 472 miles of stagecoaching, a combination that consumed 10 days.

Even after the tourists began to flow into the park, there were sticky problems in abundance. Not enough rangers were on hand to protect the geysers from vandalism, politicians gave away lucrative concessions to friends, and the "protected" game was so wantonly slaughtered, even by early park officials, that some species were nearly extinguished, most notably the buffalo. In 1886 administration was turned over to the Army, which built roads and ran the park with quiet efficiency until 1916, when the Park Service took over. Since then, affairs of this vast, complex, and over-popular park have been carried on by the Park Service and its concessioners with consummate skill.

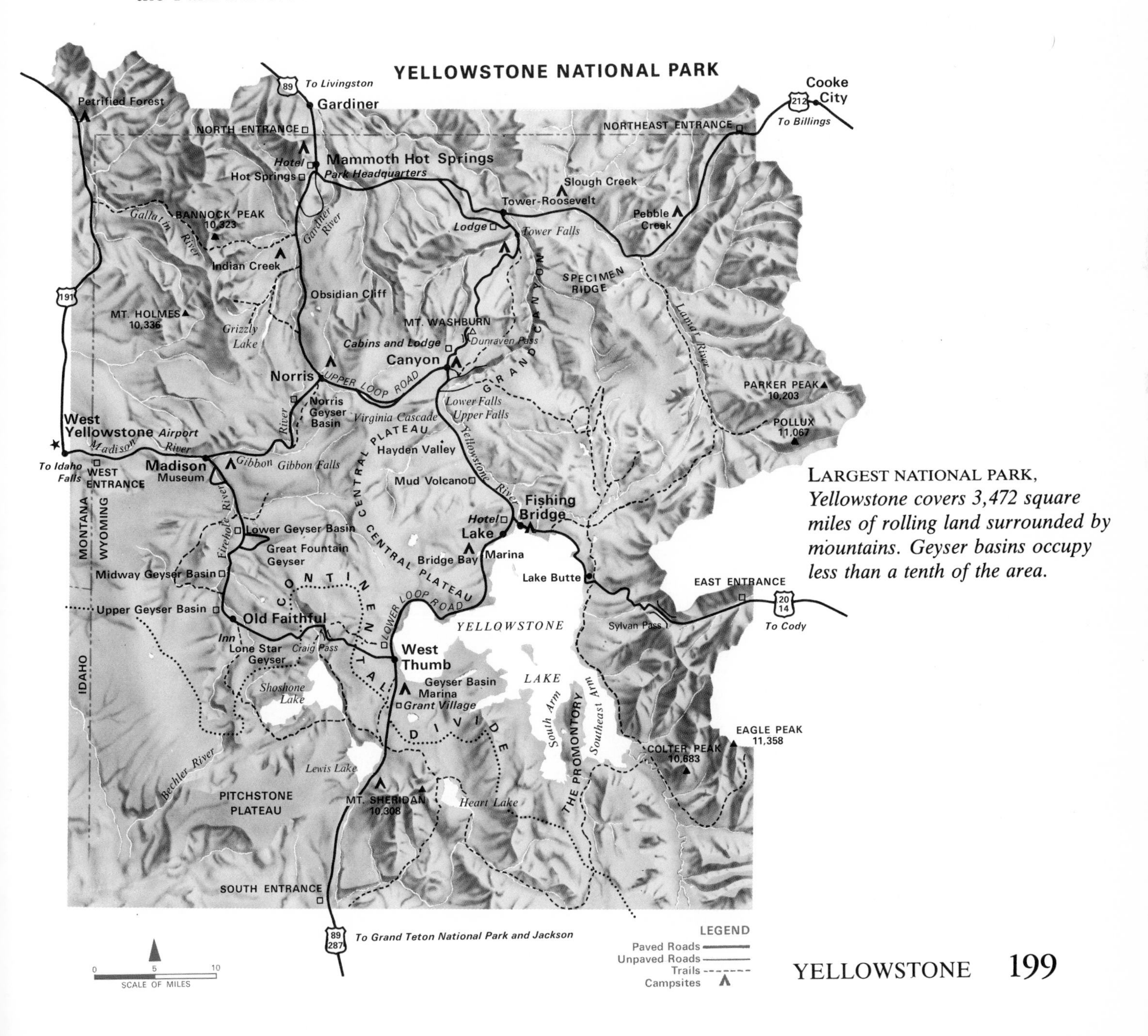

LARGEST NATIONAL PARK, *Yellowstone covers 3,472 square miles of rolling land surrounded by mountains. Geyser basins occupy less than a tenth of the area.*

Thermal Areas

THE EARTH'S INNER HEAT, close to the surface of the ground all the way across the wide plateau, is the why and wherefore of Yellowstone's renown. In many parts of the park, the ground is warm or hot to the touch, and while this heating is accomplished by heated water or gases coming up through the crust, there is every likelihood that the temperature of the rock itself reaches the melting point less than a mile below the surface. Ground water moves easily into and through the porous, fissured surface rocks, eventually working its way down to depths where temperatures far exceed the boiling point, and forming reservoirs of superheated steam. Under extreme pressure, the steam seeks a way out. It may reach the atmosphere again as a steady roaring jet that becomes visible only as it condenses to vapor some distance above the ground; then it is a steam vent, or fumarole. Or it may have its exit clogged by inflowing liquid water, which it must push out of the way; then it becomes a geyser.

A typical geyser eruption may begin with a flow, or an increase in flow, of water from the orifice, accompanied by deep-seated cannonading that seems to shake the ground and indicates that the restraining pressure is off. Then the column of water in the tube is thrown upward for a few seconds, or a few minutes, by steam that continues to rumble underground and roar skyward for some time after the water is expelled. The force of the steam jet dies down as the subterranean pressure is relieved, and water again begins to fill the exhaust tube, blocking the exit of the steam and setting the stage for the next eruption.

RICHARD ROWAN

ON THE BANK OF THE FIREHOLE RIVER, *Riverside Glacier shoots its graceful 75-foot column of water over the river for 20 minutes at intervals of 5 hours 40 minutes to 6 hours 15 minutes.*

AS IT HAS FOR THREE CENTURIES, *Old Faithful sends its towering plume of 12,000 gallons of boiling water into the thin mountain air. Famous the world over, the great geyser has attracted travelers to Yellowstone since 1870, when its existence was first reported to a disbelieving public. With reasonable faithfulness, the geyser erupts every 33 to 96 minutes for 4 or 5 minutes and then subsides. Its display is most spectacular in cool weather or early morning when the superheated water meets cold air and condenses into billowing steam.*

ROLF ZILLMER

MARTIN LITTON

SEEPING FROM THE MOUNTAINSIDE *in Mammoth Hot Springs area, hot water evaporates, leaving terraces of travertine. As terrace edges grow upward, water may break through, flowing down and outward to form new terraces. Algae colors pools and terrace edges. In background: Mammoth, with hotel in center and former Fort Yellowstone (park headquarters) at right.*

POSSIBLY THE OLDEST *of the park's geysers, Castle Geyser, named because of its fancied resemblance to the ruins of an old castle, spouts 65 to 90 feet about every 9 to 10 hours.*

RUSSELL LAMB

A GEYSER'S UNDERGROUND PLUMBING SYSTEM

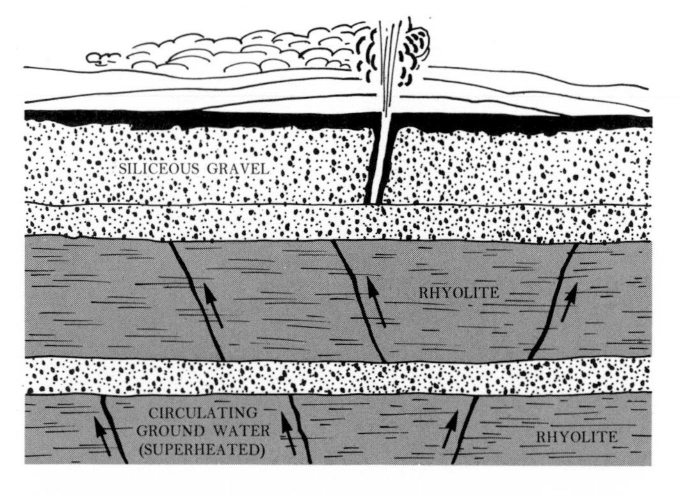

WHAT GOES ON INSIDE A GEYSER? *Water seeps down through porous volcanic soil and collects in chambers where it is turned to steam by superheated earth. The chambers all connect with a central vent which fills with water. Weight of the water in the main tube blocks escape of steam from the chambers. In time, steam is superheated to a point where it explosively expels the water in the tube into the air.*

DAVID MUENCH

RICHARD ROWAN

UNBELIEVABLE VARIETY *characterizes thermal areas of the park. Steaming Morning Glory Pool* (ABOVE) *was named in the 1880s for its remarkable likeness to the shape and color of the flower. Over the years, the temperature of the pool has dropped, allowing an edging of brown and green algae to spread toward the center.* LEFT: *Trails and boardwalks provide safe passage through active thermal areas where eerie bubblings and hissing sounds rise from below the surface.*

Back Country

HORSES AND HIKERS CAN GO over Yellowstone's gentle grades at speeds unheard of in the Sierra Nevada, Cascades, or Coast Range. The woods, waters, and wide open spaces beckon, yet the back-country trails are just beginning to be used. In the past, little or no information or encouragement was offered to facilitate wilderness trail travel, and there are still no facilities within the park for equipping parties for overnight rides or hiking trips. But this is changing rapidly. Guided horseback rides of short duration are available at several locations, and the concessioner offers week-long guided pack trips into the Gallatin Canyon area.

Most of the travel into the primitive corners of Yellowstone comes from outside the boundaries. Pack trips originating at dude ranches and pack stations around the perimeter often loop into the park, taking admirable advantage of its fine high country and productive fishing. Cooke City, 4 miles outside the Northeast Entrance, is a favorite jumping-off point for the high and rugged Absaroka Range along the east side of the park.

TO ESCAPE THE CROWDS *that come to view the park's most easily reached attractions, travel into quieter back country. Even here, summer is busy; a permit system regulates the number of campers and length of stay.*

DANIEL TYERS

DANIEL TYERS

OVER A THOUSAND MILES OF TRAILS *wind through forests, across open meadows, and alongside streams and beaver ponds. You may encounter wildlife, and in July and August, you'll see wildflowers at their best.*

HIKER MAKES A CHILLY CROSSING *of Pelican Creek east of Fishing Bridge. Elk, mule deer, and moose frequent the park's open meadowlands. Best times to see them are at dawn and in the evening.*

DANIEL TYERS

DANIEL TYERS

JAMES TALLON

EVEN FISH ARE PROTECTED *in this park where birds and animals take precedence over humans in fishing for food. Fishing is permitted, but regulations vary. Some waters are closed to fishing; some are restricted to fly fishing; in others, fish must be released with the exception of one or two that may be kept for a campfire meal.* ABOVE: *Angler escapes the crowds in a quiet area where no motor boats are permitted on the South Arm of Yellowstone Lake.* LEFT: *Clouds reflect from the surface of a serene, nameless lake in the park's northwest corner near Mammoth Hot Springs.*

The Animals

THERE IS TRUTH IN THE SAYING THAT Yellowstone National Park is the greatest wildlife sanctuary in the United States outside Alaska, but that is not so much a statement of abundance of wildlife in Yellowstone as of poverty elsewhere. Of large native animals summering on the park's 3,472 square miles, only one species—the American elk or wapiti—is numbered in the thousands (the count has been fluctuating between 10,000 and 15,000 in recent years). The populations of black bear and pronghorn seldom if ever exceed 500 each; there may be nearly a thousand mule deer and moose at times, but figures of 200 or so are probably tops for grizzly and bighorn. Yellowstone's "concentration" of bison amounts to three small herds totaling about 1,600 animals—proving that the thundering herd is indeed a thing of the past.

Beyond the range of the automobile, encounters with wildlife will be full of magic. If you recognize the deep, rolling call, you will pause to stalk a sandhill crane. If you see swans in the park in summer, you will know they are rare trumpeters; whistlers are spring and fall migrants only. If you have learned to handle a paddle efficiently and silently, the otter may let you come almost abreast of him before he dives. If you know how to stand or sit perfectly still, the curious antelope may move toward you instead of away from you. Small animals and birds are very much the same as in other mountain regions of the West.

IF YOU SEE A BEAR, DETOUR! *An adult grizzly, such as the one pictured above with her three-year-old cub, is the strongest and most ferocious mammal in North America. About 200 to 250 inhabit the park, mostly in remote back country. The park's black bears are more numerous—about 500 to 600.*

G. C. KELLEY

G. C. KELLEY

LARGEST MEMBER OF THE DEER FAMILY, *moose are seen throughout the park, often wading through marshy meadows where they feed on aquatic plants. Calves, generally twins, are born in May and remain with their mother until the following spring.*

RICHARD ROWAN

G. C. KELLEY

TWO PLAINS ANIMALS, *the bison and pronghorn, have adapted to the park environment. Both winter in lower elevations, then move to high country in summer. A few bison remain in Hayden Valley throughout the year.*

ED COOPER

GLACIER

THE INTERNATIONAL PARK

PARK FACTS: *Location:* Northwestern Montana. *Discovered:* 1800s. *Established:* National park, May 11, 1910; made part of Waterton-Glacier International Peace Park, May 22, 1932. *Size:* 1,600 sq. mi. *Altitude:* 3,154 to 10,448 ft. *Climate:* Summer days warm, nights chilly. *Season:* All year, but passes closed October-June. *Annual visitors:* 1,583,000. *Accommodations:* Campgrounds, cabins, chalets, lodges, hotels (May 15-Sept. 15). *Activities:* Boating, excursion boat cruises, golfing, horseback riding, fishing, hiking, backpacking, cross-country skiing, snowshoeing. *Information:* Supt., Glacier National Park, MT 59936.

THE MOUNTAINS OF GLACIER ARE NOT HIGH, compared with those in some national parks, but there is something distinctive about their sheer faces and angular contours that led early French explorer Pierre La Verendrye to call this "the land of shining mountains." There is something hospitable about them, too; their flanks are covered by heavy forests that descend to the edge of sapphire lakes and seem to welcome visitors. Above timberline their upper reaches are multicolored—blue-gray, buff, green, red, purple.

Straddling the Continental Divide in northwestern Montana, Glacier contains an accessible but unspoiled wilderness penetrated by 700 miles of trails. Here you can travel alone for an hour or a week, or you can take a guided trip without charge. There are saddle horses for those who want to rent them, two high mountain chalets for back country hikers, and boat cruises on park lakes.

Glacier is a land of colorful place names: Gunsight and Two Medicine are mountain passes, and Rising Wolf, Scalplock, and Going-to-the-Sun are mountains. And there are Indian names like Medicine Grizzly and Appekunny, for this is Blackfoot country. The eastern part of the park was reservation until the Blackfeet sold it in 1896. Their present home adjoins the park on the east.

This is a park that deserves ample time—time to meditate and relax, to hike and ride, to study and observe, to fish and camp. John Muir was emphatic: "Give a month at least to this precious reserve. The time will not be taken from the sum of your life. Instead of shortening, it will indefinitely lengthen it and make you truly immortal."

Glacier's northernmost boundary is on the 49th parallel, and even though its mountains reach a height of only 10,448 feet, the northern latitude means

JEWEL-LIKE GRINNELL LAKE *occupies a glacial trough below Mount Grinnell. The large glaciers that formed the terrain of the park have been gone for 10,000 years, but about 50 small glaciers still exist here.*

GLACIER NATIONAL PARK

WATERTON-GLACIER INTERNATIONAL PEACE PARK *is the only park in the world to cross an international boundary and include land in two countries. The park straddles the Continental Divide. Only one road crosses it, but a railroad and highway skirt the southern edge. Spur roads lead to the park resorts.*

abundant snow. The snowfall and dozens of glaciers within the park feed more than 200 lakes and rushing streams. Water seems to be everywhere, in lush verdant valleys, in meadows ablaze with wildflowers, along roads, and nestling in glacial cirques at the base of sheer rock walls. Water is so abundant that the visitor is seldom out of sight of a lake or out of hearing of a waterfall or stream.

Although this is a trail park of the first magnitude, the scenic Going-to-the-Sun Road is one of the most spectacular drives in America. The roads within the park are not generally passable much before June 15, but if weather permits they are kept open until mid-October.

Adjoining Glacier on the north is Canada's Waterton Lakes National Park, and together they form the Waterton-Glacier International Peace Park, dedicated in 1932 to the permanent peace and friendship of the two neighboring nations. By all means, cross the boundary for a visit to the Canadian park. No passport is necessary for U.S. citizens, and the boat trips, fine food, and English shops will remain in your memory as a pleasant adjunct to your Glacier trip.

ROLF ZILLMER

HIKERS ON HIGHLAND TRAIL *head for the famous flower banks of the Garden Wall. The avocet* (BELOW LEFT), *a striking black-and-white bird, is sometimes seen in the park's marshes and ponds. The ptarmigan* (BELOW RIGHT), *seen here in winter garb, frequents wooded areas. Its snowy coat changes to brown in summer.*

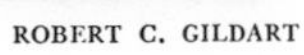

ROBERT C. GILDART

ROBERT C. GILDART

IN EARLY MORNING MIST, *Swiftcurrent Lake takes on an unreal look. Glacier's lakes invite boating. You can launch your own boat; rent a rowboat, canoe, or motor boat; or board a sleek launch for a scenic tour of Swiftcurrent, St. Mary, Waterton, or Two Medicine lakes, or Lake McDonald.*

ROLF ZILLMER

PEAKS OF GARDEN WALL *rise in brooding majesty along the spine of the Continental Divide. This sweeping view, encompassing acres of glacier lilies, looks north from Logan Pass.*

DAVID MUENCH

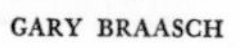
GARY BRAASCH

FURRY "VELVET," *containing nourishment-providing blood vessels, sheathes antlers of mule deer. He'll rub off this soft tissue in late summer after his antlers have hardened. Antlers will be shed after the fall mating season, regrown next summer.*

AT SUNRISE, *the Sinopah Mountains, mirrored in calm Two Medicine Lake, look like a stage set. Conical-shaped and richly colored, the peak in the foreground is aptly named Painted Teepee.*

RUSSELL LAMB

CLOUDS SWEEP THE SUMMITS *of Heavy Runner Peak (left in photograph) and Reynolds Mountain beyond it. View is from a vantage point above Going-to-the-Sun Road east of Logan Pass.* RUSSELL LAMB

LACY COW PARSNIP *and brilliant fireweed enliven a sunlit grove of aspens near St. Mary Lake. Elk, bears, and other animals find the cow parsnip to their liking—when not browsed, it can grow to 8 feet tall.*

RUSSELL LAMB

MOUNT McKINLEY

HOME OF THE INVISIBLE MOUNTAIN

PARK FACTS: *Location:* South central Alaska. *Discovered:* 1896. *Established:* February 26, 1917. *Size:* 3,030 sq. mi. *Altitude:* 1,400-20,320 ft. *Climate:* Cool, wet, and windy. *Season:* May 15 to September 15. *Annual visitors:* 461,000. *Accommodations:* Hotel, campgrounds. *Activities:* Hiking, wildlife tours, ice climbing (registration required for mountains over 10,000 ft.). *Information:* Supt., McKinley Park, AK 99755.

MOUNT MCKINLEY, THE HIGHEST MOUNTAIN IN NORTH AMERICA, lies only 250 miles south of the Arctic Circle. Guarding the Alaska Range with its neighbor Mount Foraker, this great peak rises to the sublime height of 20,320 feet. Small wonder the Indians of the region called it *Denali* (The High One).

Mount McKinley National Park is one of America's largest parks, and in its 3,030 square miles man has intruded but slightly. There is only one road and one area of major development.

Long before you reach the park, you can see the glacier-mantled mountain, stark and foreboding, a giant among giants. The first glimpse from within the park is at a point 8 miles from McKinley Park Station, but the mountain does not appear in its full glory until the last 25 or 30 miles. The views are less obstructed here, and although the summit is still more than 20 miles from the road at its nearest point, it appears so near that one feels a hiker could reach the snowy slopes in a 10-minute walk. Unfortunately, the mountain is not visible from the hotel.

Probably the best view, and certainly the most photographed, is from near the end of the road, with Wonder Lake in the foreground. Mount McKinley is a stunning sight at midday, when the sunlight glistens on its snow and glaciers, but at sunrise or during the long subarctic twilight it is magnificent. Then delicate pastel shades enshroud it, changing with every shift of light, softening and transforming it from a great mass of granite, ice, and snow into a thing of ethereal beauty.

Weather is the enemy of visitors to this park. Summers are cool and windy, and you can count on rain half the time. You can be in the area for days and never see the mountain at all because of low-hanging clouds. Yet, even when

THE PARK'S MAIN SPECTACLE, *magnificent Mount McKinley dominates a great wilderness 250 miles south of the Arctic Circle. Highest peak on the North American continent, it rises spectacularly from only 2,000 feet above sea level to 20,320 feet.*

MALCOLM LOCKWOOD

the mountain is not visible, there is much else of interest. The park is a sanctuary for wildlife, and you can see many animals from the road – especially if you use field glasses.

The mighty Toklat grizzly is frequently seen. Moose are common and are usually seen browsing in willow thickets. The annual migratory route of the barren-ground caribou, close relative of the domesticated reindeer, crosses the park. For a few days in late June and early July hundreds of these animals can be seen moving leisurely over the slopes and along the river bottoms. It is difficult to determine exactly when the migration will occur, and you can count yourself extremely fortunate if you are in the right place during the short time it is visible from the road.

Most of the park lies above timberline. In this northern latitude timberline ranges between 2,500 and 3,000 feet. Alpine tundra, not to be confused with arctic tundra, covers much of the park. It is of two types, wet and dry. Wet tundra is characterized by a luxuriant growth of grasses, mosses, lichens, and low shrubs. Small ponds frequently dot this dense mat, and hiking is difficult. Dry tundra is typical of higher, well-drained soils, but it is composed of dwarf plant forms.

The park road varies in elevation from 1,600 feet at the entrance to about 4,000 feet near Eielson Visitor Center. It is hilly and winding. For most of its 87 miles, it is gravel-surfaced. During the visitor season, private vehicles are not permitted beyond Savage River, 14 miles from the park entrance, except to proceed to campsites. Free buses run regularly from the Visitor Orientation Center at Riley Creek to Eielson Visitor Center and on to Wonder Lake, stopping at key points along the park road.

Alaska Highway 3 provides access to the park from Fairbanks (120 miles) and Anchorage (240 miles). The Alaska Railroad follows much the same route and takes passengers almost to the door of the hotel. In summer the park can be reached from Paxson along the gravel-surfaced Denali Highway.

The park was established in 1917 primarily to protect wildlife from extinction by an army of hunters that was expected to arrive when the Alaska Railroad was completed to the area. Conservation groups, such as the Boone and Crockett Club of New York and the Campfire Club of America, worked under the leadership of the "Father of McKinley Park," Charles Sheldon, to persuade Congress to establish the park, which it did six years before the rails reached it.

Another reason for creating the park was to establish a reserve around the largest mountain on the continent. The "High One," known to explorers and prospectors for a century, was officially named in 1897 for President McKinley by a prospector named W. A. Dickey, who bestowed the name in a fit of exasperation. After spending several weary days listening to a pair of fellow prospectors advance arguments in favor of free silver, he chose in retaliation to name the peak for the leading advocate of the gold standard.

TYPICAL OF THE LAKES *that abound in the wilderness around Mount McKinley, this one near the park's East Entrance mirrors the quiet scene around its shores. It is a favorite haunt of moose and waterfowl.*

JON GARDEY

AUTUMN COLORS THE SCENE *in this view from the Fairbanks-Anchorage Highway near the park entrance. The brilliant show will end all too soon beneath the first snows of the long Alaska winter.*

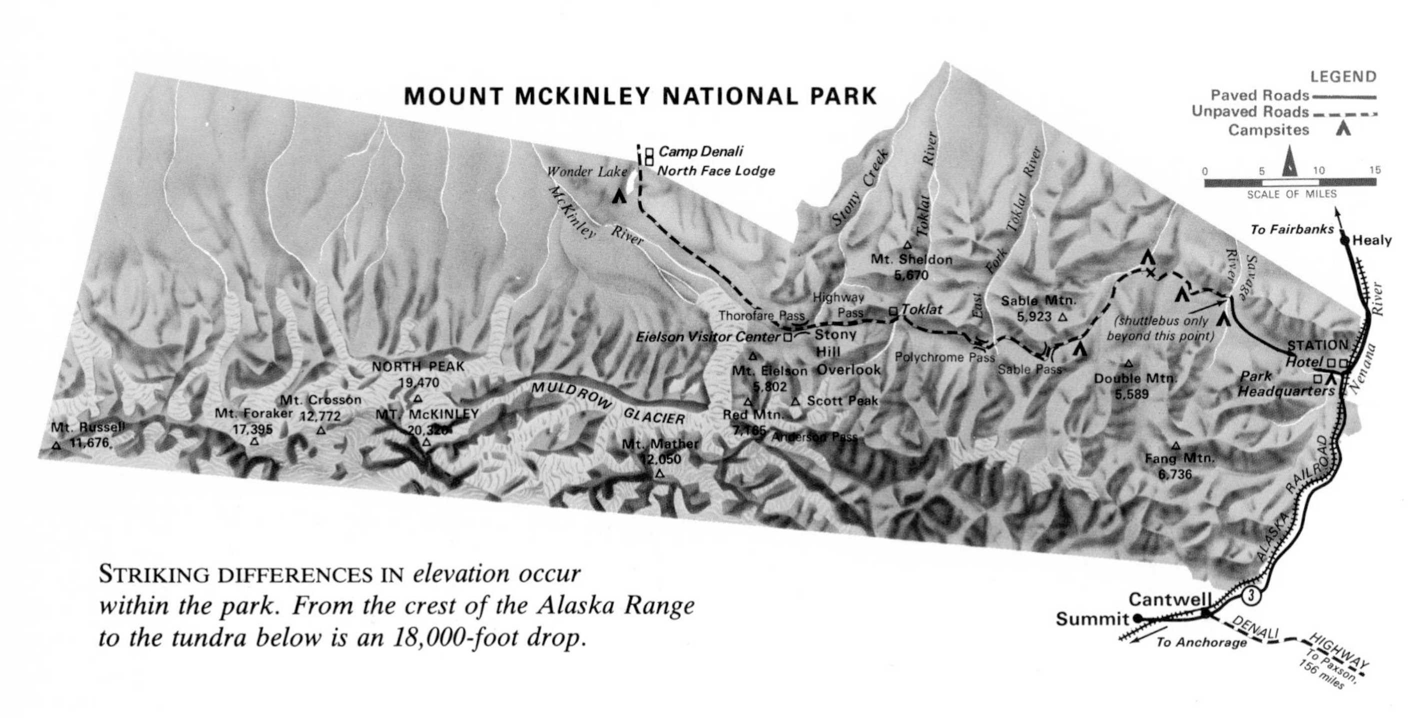

STRIKING DIFFERENCES IN *elevation occur within the park. From the crest of the Alaska Range to the tundra below is an 18,000-foot drop.*

MALCOLM LOCKWOOD

UNDAUNTED *by an early snowfall, a colorful Alaska Railroad train brings freight and passengers to the park station—an 8-hour trip from Anchorage, 4 hours from Fairbanks.*

MALCOLM LOCKWOOD

G. C. KELLEY

EVENLY MATCHED *bull moose lock horns in mating-season battle. These encounters look and sound ferocious but serious injury seldom results. A trio of aloof caribou* (BELOW) *parades across the tundra. Caribou winter outside the park and return to it in spring, following general route patterns within a region 200 to 300 miles in diameter and traveling several hundred miles in their annual circuit.*

MARK MCDERMOTT

MARK MCDERMOTT

UNIQUE AMONG MCKINLEY NATIVES *are the Dall sheep that roam in bands over the higher slopes. At home on slippery talus, they are relatively safe on steep slopes from attack by less sure-footed predators. These ewes and lambs seem unperturbed by the proximity of the young boys sharing their hillside.*

NANCY RABENER

MARK MCDERMOTT

FLUFFY PUFFS OF "COTTON" *top grasslike sedge. The soft white balls are actually silky hairs that grow from the spikes of inconspicuous flowers and help to disperse seeds.*

WHEN THE CLOUDS COOPERATE, *Mount McKinley and the beautiful peaks of the Alaska Range look close enough to touch. Named "Denali" (the High One) by the Indians, the mountain was renamed for President McKinley in 1896 by William A. Dickey, a prospector.*

ALASKA'S NEW PARKS (proposed)

THE NATION'S LAST GREAT WILDERNESS

PARK FACTS: *Location:* 13 areas throughout state of Alaska. *Area:* 43,000,000 to 44,000,000 acres. *Accommodations (Denali, Glacier Bay, Katmai):* Campgrounds, cabins, lodges. *Information:* National Park Service, Alaska Area Office, 540 W. 5th Ave., Anchorage, AK 99501.

ALASKA, LARGEST STATE IN THE UNION, spans four time zones and boasts of our country's highest mountains, longest scenic rivers, more than half of our coastline, and most of our dwindling wildlife. Most of the state's lands appear virtually unmarked, affected only by seasons, weather, the descent of a glacier down a mountain valley, or the migration of a caribou herd across the tundra.

At press time Congress is considering park and preserve status for 13 existing national monuments. Added would be such scenic splendors as Aniakchak, a spectacle of volcanism; Bering Land Bridge, one-time link between Asia and North America; Cape Krusenstern, an archeological treasury; Gates of the Arctic, encompassing north and south slopes of the Brooks Range; Kenai Fjords, a land of ice; Kobuk Valley, Alaska's sandy Sahara; Lake Clark, spectacular meeting spot of the Alaska and Aleutian ranges; Noatak, crossroads for caribou; Wrangell-St. Elias, a gigantic collection of the continent's greatest peaks and glaciers; and Yukon-Charley, with its gold rush history and river resources.

Because the land is relatively unproductive and fragile, Alaska's parks must be large. One arctic grizzly needs 100 square miles just to feed itself and rear its young. With the passage of the parks bill, acreage will be added to Katmai and Glacier Bay to preserve entire ecosystems. Mt. McKinley National Park will be enlarged by Denali's 4,000,000 acres, protecting the habitat of large mammals and the entire mountain's geological formation.

Some of the parks are easier to visit than others. Previously developed areas such as Glacier Bay and Katmai offer visitor facilities and also include guided tours of their scenic specialties. Many of the parks, reached only by bush plane or avid backpacker, will remain much as they always have—places for scenic solitude and scientific study.

"THE TUSK" *juts skyward from the mountain grandeur of the Chigmit Mountains southwest of Anchorage. Two low passes, Merrill and Lake Clark, penetrate this land of sheer-walled canyons, waterfalls, and a mountain range that contains two active volcanoes over 10,000 feet high.*

JOHN & MARGARET IBBOTSON/ALASKA PHOTO

GREAT TRAILLESS EXPANSES *offer unforgettable experiences to those who are willing to accept nature on her own terms.* RIGHT: *A full moon illuminates the awesome terrain of Ruth Gorge, Denali National Monument.* BELOW: *Hiker in Arrigetch Peaks, Gates of the Arctic National Monument, pauses to enjoy a quiet view. Hikers and backpackers heading into these valleys generally arrange to be dropped off and picked up by chartered aircraft.*

GALEN ROWELL

ELLIOTT VARNER SMITH

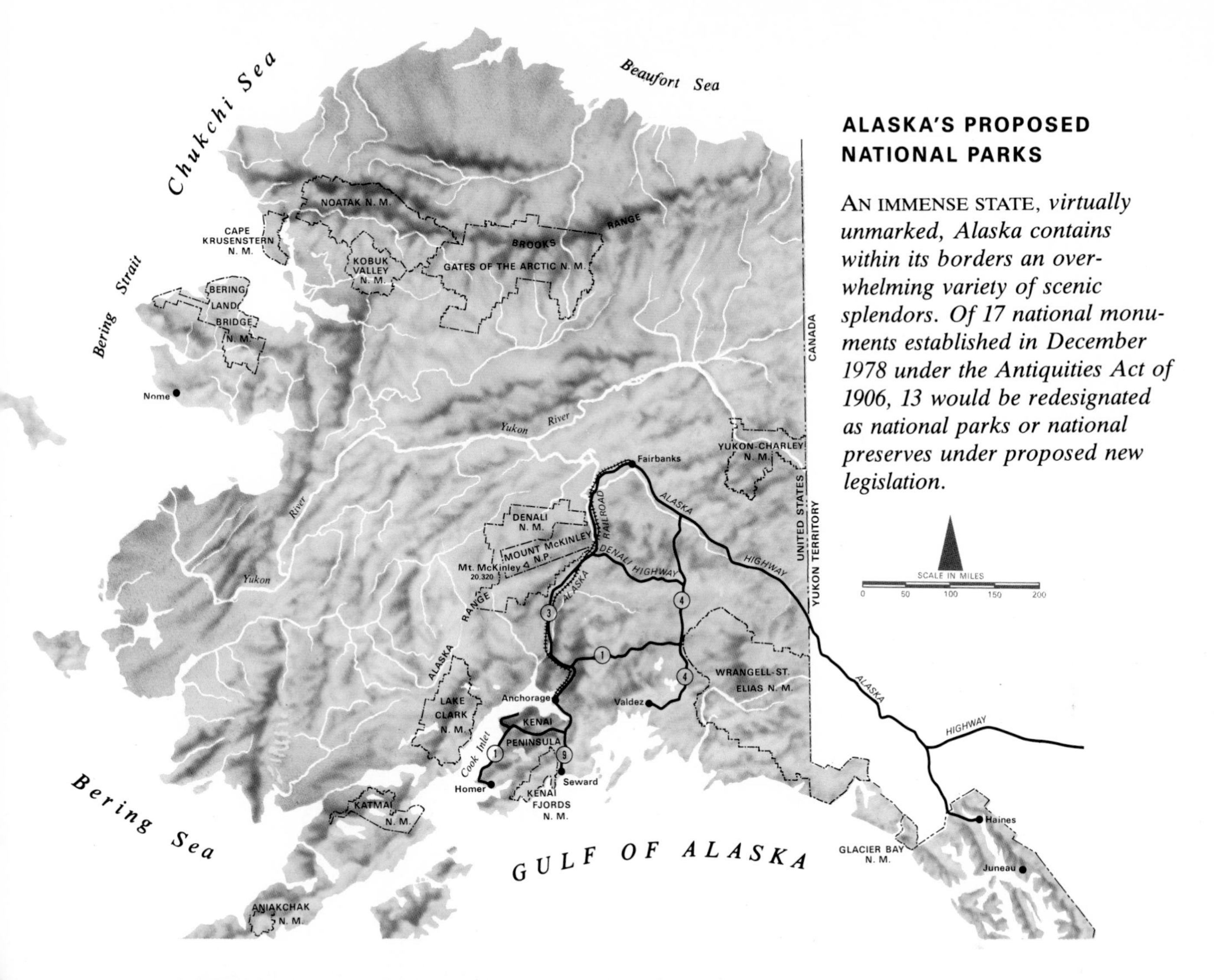

ALASKA'S PROPOSED NATIONAL PARKS

AN IMMENSE STATE, *virtually unmarked, Alaska contains within its borders an overwhelming variety of scenic splendors. Of 17 national monuments established in December 1978 under the Antiquities Act of 1906, 13 would be redesignated as national parks or national preserves under proposed new legislation.*

WILDERNESS RECREATION *and easy access from Anchorage (1½ hours by chartered plane) bring several thousand visitors to Lake Clark annually. The monument provides habitat for a variety of wildlife. The 50-mile segment bordering Cook Inlet contains some 100 bird species, including the endangered peregrine falcon and 11 varieties of waterfowl.*

JIM FARO/ALASKA PHOTO

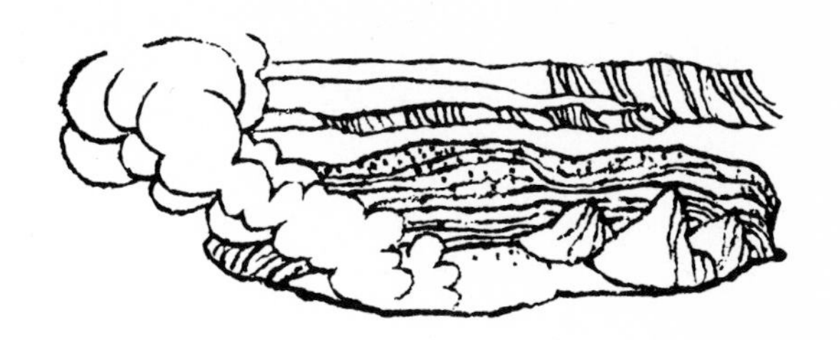

HAWAII VOLCANOES

HOME OF THE VOLCANO GODDESS

PARK FACTS: *Location:* Southeastern Hawaii. *Discovered:* By missionaries in 1830s. *Established:* Hawaii National Park, August 1, 1916; Haleakala separated from park, 1961; renamed Hawaii Volcanoes. *Size:* 344 sq. mi. *Altitude:* Sea level to 13,677 ft. *Climate:* From semitropical to snowy (on Mauna Loa). *Season:* All year. *Annual visitors:* 2,322,000. *Accommodations:* Campgrounds, cabins, hotel. *Activities:* Backpacking, guided tours. *Information:* Supt., Hawaii Volcanoes National Park, HI 96718.

THE EIGHTEEN HAWAIIAN ISLANDS are actually the tips of a massive range of volcanic mountains that rise from the bottom of the Pacific. They formed slowly, in the way of shield volcanoes: Liquid lava erupted and spread in broad sheets; as these hardened to build up successive layers, great inverted saucers or "shields" took shape. Thus over the ages the mountains grew up from the ocean floor, until their peaks finally rose above the surface of the sea.

They were not all created at the same time. The big island of Hawaii is the youngest, and on it are found the only volcanoes in the range that are still active: Mauna Loa and Kilauea. These two are among the most exciting in existence, and their crests are the principal features of Hawaii Volcanoes National Park.

Mauna Loa, "Long Mountain," is in fact the biggest mountain in the world, although most of it is hidden under the waters of the Pacific. Its base is on the ocean floor, and the lower 18,000 feet of its elevation lie below the water. The summit is 13,677 feet above sea level, so its total size is astonishing: a mass 100 times that of Mount Shasta, a height more than 2,000 feet greater than that of Mount Everest.

Mauna Loa has a large crater or caldera, called Mokuaweoweo. Within this great basin are several summit craters that have erupted in the past and partially covered the caldera floor with lava.

Although smaller than Mauna Loa, Kilauea gets even more attention because it is so accessible. Visitors can park their cars within 200 feet of its summit or drive all the way around the top on good roads. At some time in the past the mountaintop collapsed to form a small caldera, or cauldron, and within this basin

FOUNTAIN OF FIRE *flares up 1,000 feet from the crater of Kilauea. In the first stages of an eruption, fire fountains break through the lava crust, then are followed by a flood of fiery lava.*

ROBERT WENKAM

is a small crater called Halemaumau, or "Fern House."

Prior to 1924, a lake of molten lava constantly rose and fell inside Halemaumau; and within recent years, the crater has provided some of the most dramatic demonstrations to be seen anywhere. Wild fountains spray upward, and lava pours out of cracks in the floor.

This is the legendary home of Pele, the Hawaiian goddess of volcanoes. She is gone a good deal, visiting other islands of the Pacific; but Hawaiians always know when she returns, because of renewed activity in Halemaumau.

Eruptions within the craters of Mauna Loa and Kilauea are relatively harmless, extremely exciting, and fascinating to watch—and thousands of spectators have looked in on them from the crater rims. But the eruptions also break out in other areas. Both of the volcanoes have huge fissures in their flanks, and when underground pressures grow great enough to force the lava out these openings, it starts a slow and deadly advance down the slopes toward the sea, destroying crops and villages in its path. In 1960 the village of Kapoho was buried.

The active interest of Hawaiian citizens in protecting and preserving their volcanoes led to establishment in 1916 of Hawaii National Park. It included not only portions of Mauna Loa and Kilauea but also part of Haleakala, on the island of Maui. In 1961 the Haleakala section became a separate national park, and the Mauna Loa-Kilauea section was given its present name.

TWO GREAT VOLCANOES, *Mauna Loa and Kilauea, dominate the park's terrain. Formed by gentle outpourings of lava over the centuries, they are shaped like inverted saucers. Within each massive caldera are smaller craters.*

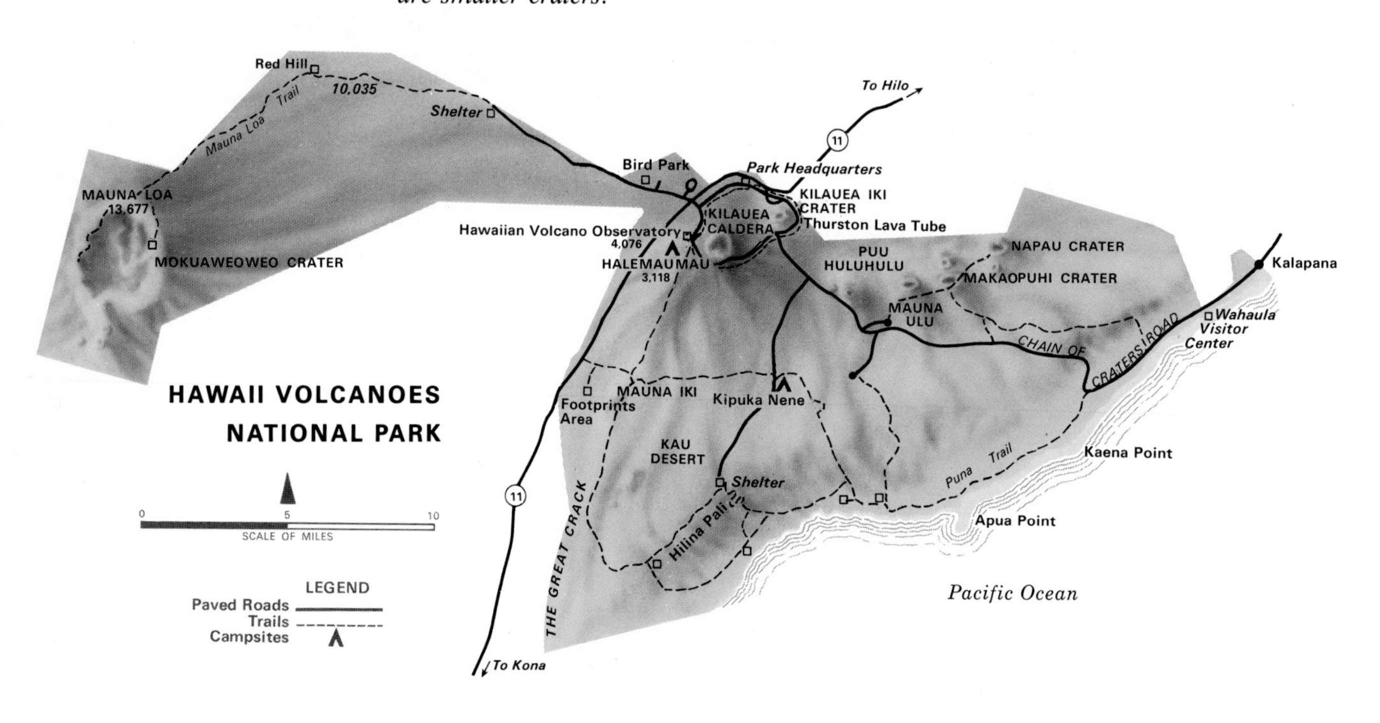

JOHN I. KJARGAARD

SUMMIT OF MAUNA LOA, *25 miles away from Kilauea, is 10,000 feet higher.* BELOW: *In contrast to the bleak expanse of lava, a tangle of ferns, some as large as small trees, share a jungle luxuriance with scrubby ohia trees in the eastern part of the park.*

ED COOPER

JOHN I. KJARGAARD

CALLED THE "DRIVE-IN VOLCANO" *because of its easy-to-reach action, a Kilauea eruption attracts crowds of people who come for the good, close-up views of fountains, lakes, rivers, and falls of molten lava.*

JOHN I. KJARGAARD

JOHN I. KJARGAARD

THE SEA STEAMS *as hot lava cascades into it following an eruption of Kilauea.* LEFT: *Wahaula Visitor Center, at the Kalapana entrance to the park, adjoins the ruins of Wahaula Heiau, where ruling chiefs once prayed and held human sacrifices. From a starting point near the heiau, a 1¼-mile hiking trail follows a circle route to the sea.*

HALEAKALA

THE MOON ON EARTH

PARK FACTS: *Location:* East Maui, Hawaiian Islands. *Established:* Part of Hawaii National Park, August 1, 1916; separate status, July 1, 1961. *Size:* 45 sq. mi. *Altitude:* Sea level to 10,023 ft. *Climate:* Cool, often foggy at high elevations; warm, humid, sunny on coast. *Season:* All year. *Annual visitors:* 740,000. *Accommodations:* Primitive campgrounds, cabins. *Activities:* Hiking, guided horseback trips, backpacking, swimming (Kipahulu section). *Information:* Supt., Haleakala National Park, Box 537, Makawao, HI 96768.

MOST OF THE EASTERN PART of the Hawaiian island of Maui is a weirdly beautiful wasteland created by the fiery outpourings of a huge, now dormant volcano. The sleeping giant is called Haleakala: "House of the Sun."

At sea level the great mountain is 33 miles long and 24 miles wide. The elevation at its summit is 10,023 feet—high enough for snow flurries in winter. From the glassed-in Puu Ulaula Observatory at the top, visitors can see as far as 130 miles on clear days. In one direction the slope drops away to the sea; in another, the distant peaks of Mauna Loa and Mauna Kea, on the island of Hawaii, are visible. And in the foreground is the curious landscape of the vast Haleakala Crater, its floor 3,000 feet below the summit, its circumference 21 miles.

The bowl is pocked with numerous smaller craters and studded with cones formed of the cinders, ash, and spatter blown from volcanic vents. The tallest of these multicolored forms, Puu O Maui, rises about 600 feet above the surrounding landscape.

Although Haleakala has not been active since the mid-eighteenth century, it is considered dormant rather than extinct; one indication that it is not dead is the earthquake activity recorded periodically on Maui.

There are several good vantage points along the rim drive to the summit, including Leleiwi and Kalahaku overlooks and the Haleakala Visitor Center. All look across to the peak called Hanakauhi, "Maker of Mists," which is often wreathed in clouds.

Most of the crater is nearly barren of plant life, but in the northeast corner is a surprise—an oasis of trees, grasses, and ferns. This spot receives 150 to 200 inches of rain a year, and the soil conditions are right for vegetation. Some

REFLECTING THE SUN'S RAYS *in a constantly changing array of colors, cinder cones in Haleakala crater create scenes that range from monotonous to brightly colored. The cones, formed by grains of iron oxide lava, reflect the rays differently as time of day and weather change.*

JOSEF MUENCH

plants exist elsewhere in the crater: one is the rare silversword, found only on the islands of Maui and Hawaii. When this odd plant matures (within 4 to 20 years) with a tall, fat stalk, it bears hundreds of small, purplish flowers. After blooming, it dies.

Two main trails lead into Haleakala Crater, where they branch into a network that totals about 30 miles. Hikers and horseback riders will find many exotic volcanic formations, a colorful part of the trail called Pele's Paintpot, and on a cross trail, Pele's Pig Pen (a half-buried spatter vent). Stone monuments left by the early Hawaiians are also of interest.

Haleakala was included (along with Mauna Loa and Kilauea on the island of Hawaii) in Hawaii National Park when it was established in 1916. In 1961, a division of that park resulted in redesignating the Mauna Loa-Kilauea section

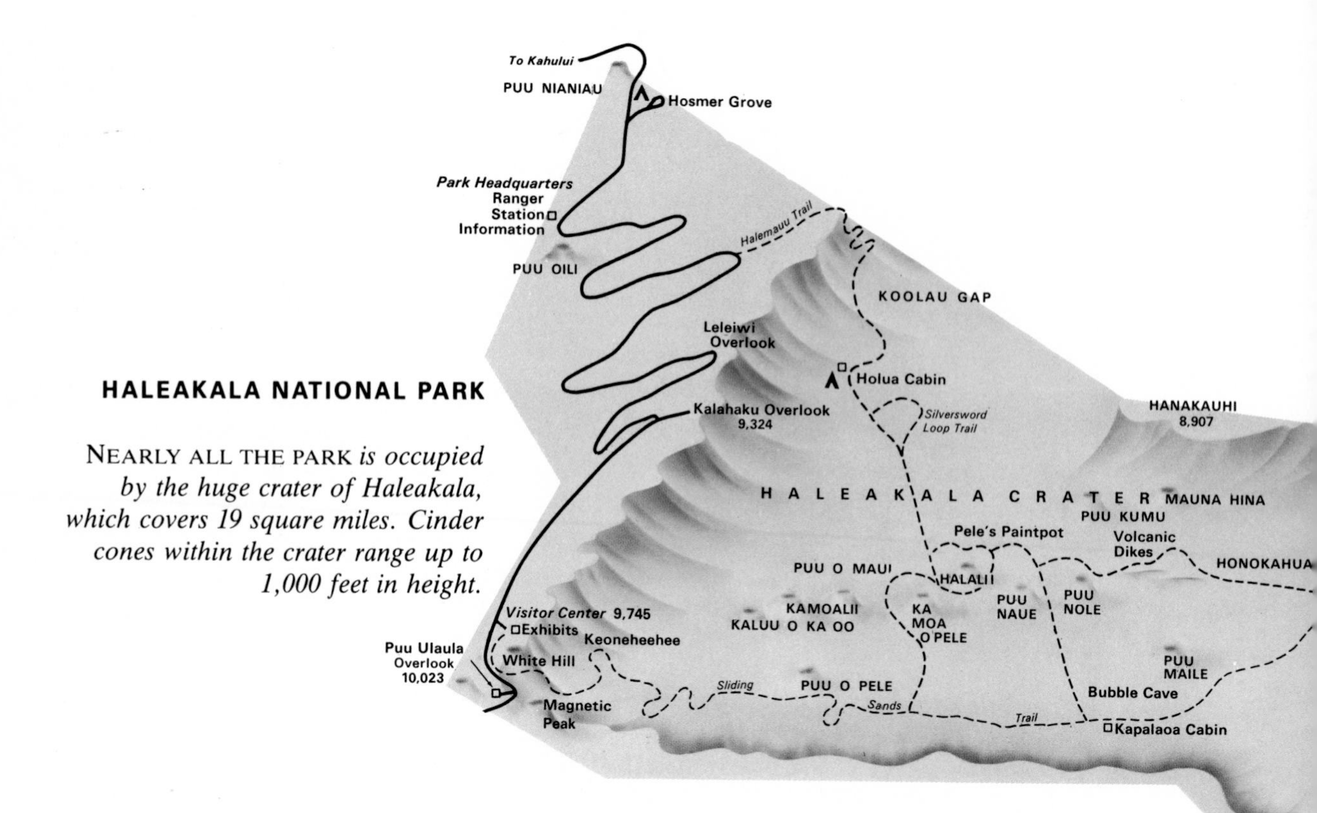

HALEAKALA NATIONAL PARK

NEARLY ALL THE PARK *is occupied by the huge crater of Haleakala, which covers 19 square miles. Cinder cones within the crater range up to 1,000 feet in height.*

as Hawaii Volcanoes National Park and the Maui section as Haleakala National Park. A major portion of the Kipahulu Valley on the eastern side of the mountain was added to the park in 1969.

In the Hosmer Grove, Paliku, and rain forest areas of the park, there are birds in surprising number and variety. A dozen kinds of introduced birds share the sanctuary with natives; the rare nene (Hawaiian goose) has been reintroduced to the island after nearing extinction. No mammals are native to the park, but there are some immigrant pigs, goats, and smaller animals.

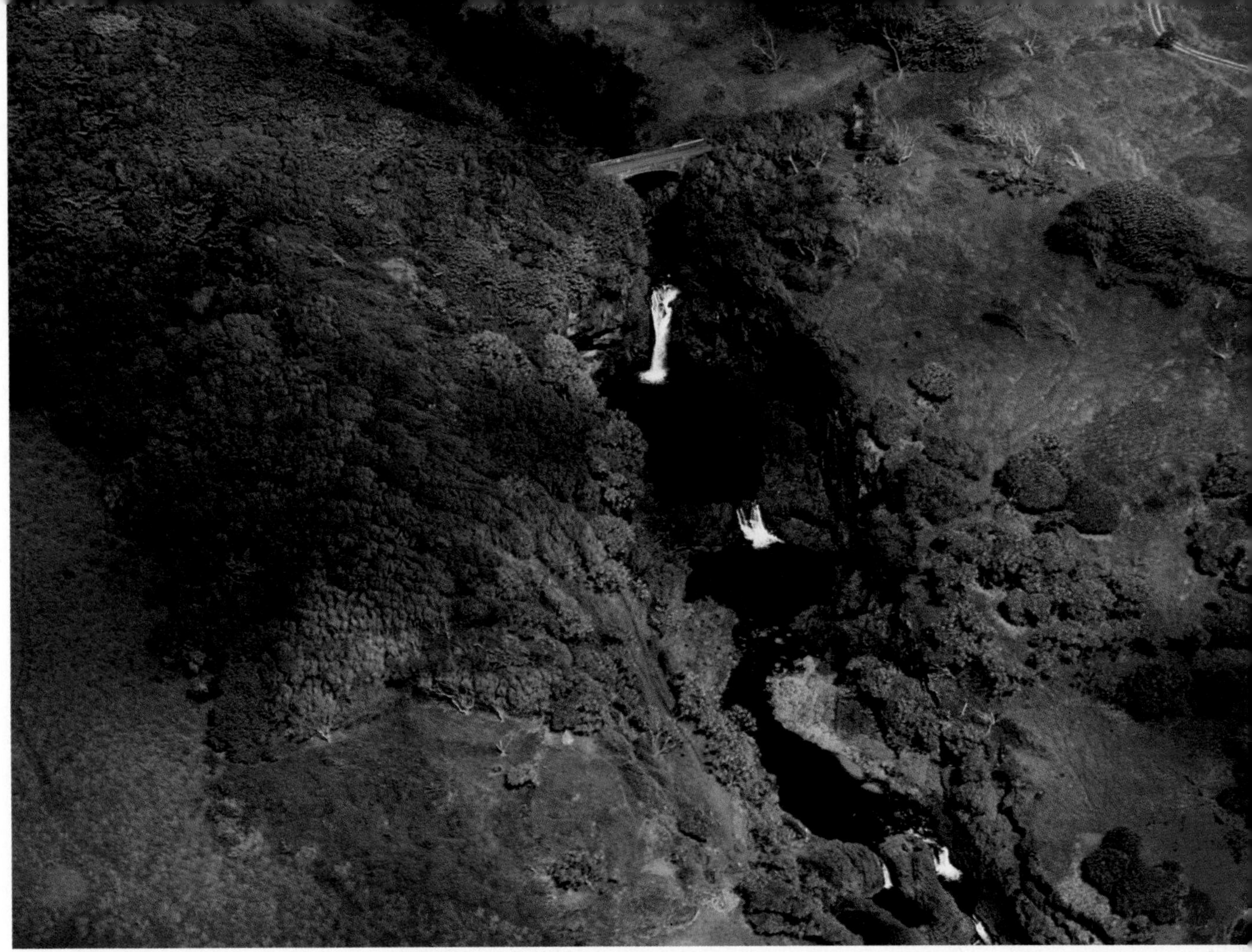

JOHN I. KJARGAARD

KIPAHULU VALLEY *has virgin forest of rare native plants above 3,000 feet. At lower elevations, Oheo Stream tumbles seaward in a series of picturesque pools above and below Oheo Bridge.*

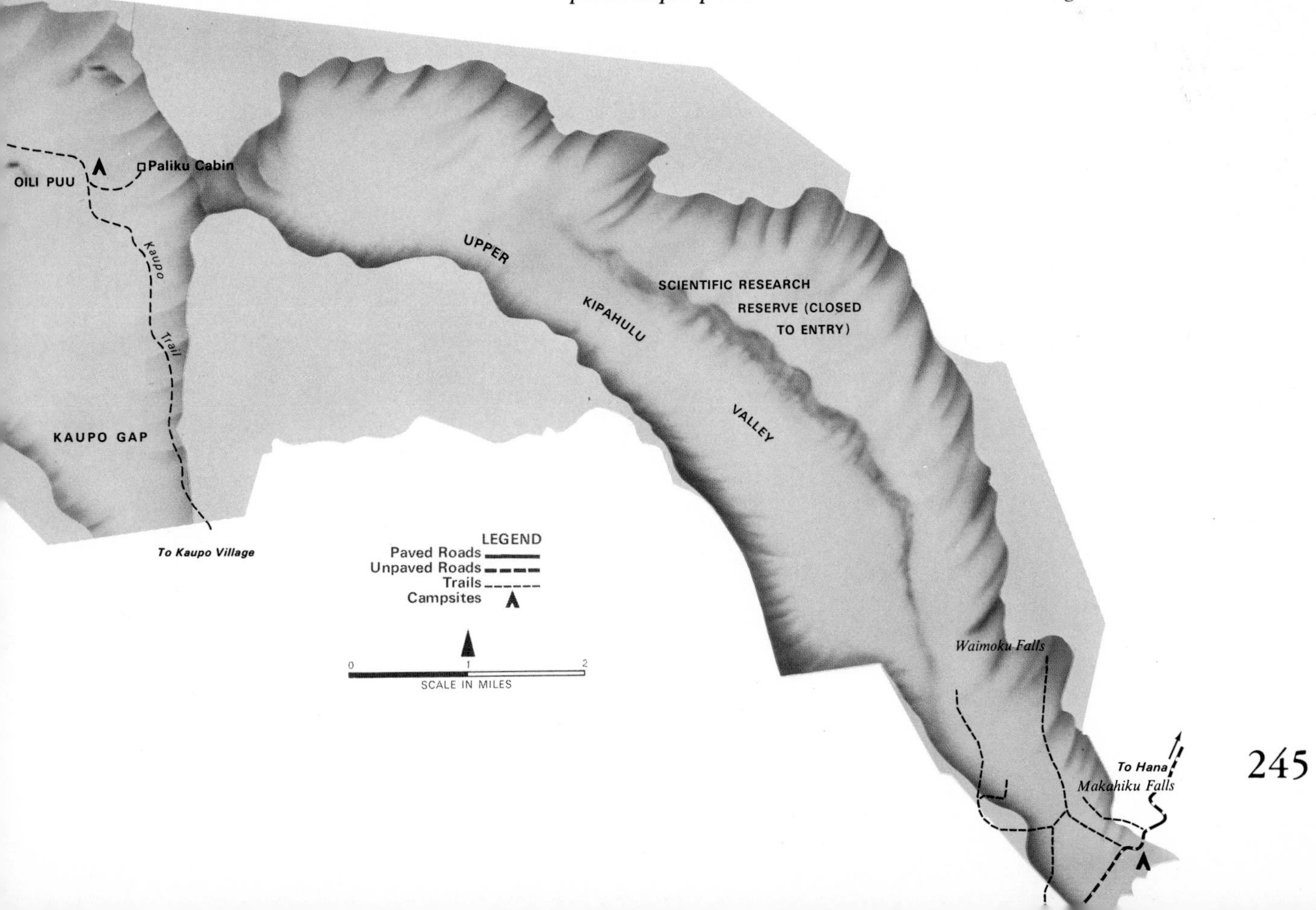

RADLAUER PRODUCTIONS, INC.

HARALD SUND

DWARFED BY THE MOONLIKE LANDSCAPE, *a trio of hikers climbs the trail among cinder cones and other curiosities, including the silversword* (ABOVE) *—a rare plant that grows for 4 to 20 years, sends up a single flower stalk in a brief burst of bloom, then dies.*

INSIDE THE CRATER, *Paliku Cabin nestles in a tiny green oasis at the base of cinder-strewn slopes. Three crater cabins, Kapalaoa, Paliku, and Holua, offer rustic accommodations and a chance for visitors to experience the eerie, nighttime world within the crater.*

JOHN I. KJARGAARD

RAY MAINS

AT RAINY PALIKU, *large native trees, tall grass, and ferns create a cool, green haven for horses and riders on a guided overnight ride.*

National Monuments

and other Park Service areas

In addition to national parks, there are 93 national monuments, recreation areas, historic sites, and memorials in the West, all administered by the National Park Service. Each is briefly described below. The post office address, attractions, facilities, and activities are listed. Unless otherwise stated, further information about any of these areas may be obtained by writing to the superintendent at the address listed.

NORTHWEST

Coulee Dam National Recreation Area, Coulee Dam, WA 99116. Franklin D. Roosevelt Lake, with 660 miles of lakeshore, offers water-oriented recreation. Campgrounds, fuel, swimming, boating, water-skiing, fishing.

Fort Clatsop National Memorial, Astoria, OR 97103. Historic encampment site of Lewis-Clark expedition during winter of 1805-6.

Fort Vancouver National Historic Site, Vancouver, WA 98661. Western headquarters of the Hudson's Bay Company from 1825 to 1860, and the first military post in the Northwest. Reconstructed buildings, museum.

John Day Fossil Beds National Monument, John Day, OR 97845. Plant and animal fossils from five epochs are displayed at three separate sites. Campground.

Lake Chelan National Recreation Area, Sedro Woolley, WA 98284. At the southern end of North Cascades National Park, Lake Chelan NRA contains the lush Stehekin Valley and a portion of fjordlike Lake Chelan. Accessible by floatplane, boat, trail. Campgrounds, hotel, meals, fuel, boating, fishing, horseback riding.

Oregon Caves National Monument, Cave Junction, OR 97523. Intricate flowstone formations ornament marble cavern. Hotel, cabins, meals, guided tours through caves.

Ross Lake National Recreation Area, Sedro Woolley, WA 98284. Separating the north and south units of North Cascades National Park, Ross Lake offers boating and hiking in a scenic reservoir ringed by mountains. Campgrounds, boat-in campsites, hotel, meals, boating, fishing.

San Juan Island National Historical Park, Friday Harbor, WA 98250. Commemorates the mid-19th century dispute between Britain and the United States over ownership of San Juan Island. Camps on both ends of the island have been preserved; three original buildings at English Camp have been restored.

Whitman Mission National Historic Site, Walla Walla, WA 99362. Landmark on the Oregon Trail, mission was the site where Dr. and Mrs. Marcus Whitman ministered to Indians.

CALIFORNIA

Cabrillo National Monument, San Diego, CA 92106. Memorial to Juan Rodriguez Cabrillo, discoverer and explorer of western United States. Includes old Point Loma Lighthouse, built in 1854. Gray whales migrate offshore from December through February.

Channel Islands National Monument, Ventura, CA 93003. This chain of islands off the Southern California coast supports large numbers of sea lions, sea birds, and unique plants. Campgrounds and commercial transportation are available for visitors to Anacapa and Santa Barbara islands; private boaters can obtain a permit to land on San Miguel island.

DEATH VALLEY NATIONAL MONUMENT, Death Valley, CA 92328. Vast desert in California and Nevada contains sand dunes, salt flats, borax formations, and other desert phenomena. Includes the lowest point in the Western Hemisphere, and Scotty's Castle, lavish desert mansion built by a prospector. Campgrounds, hotel, meals, fuel, horseback trips, golf.

DEVILS POSTPILE NATIONAL MONUMENT, Sequoia and Kings Canyon National Parks, CA 93271. Organlike pipes of blue-gray basalt rise 60 feet in columns formed by hot lava nearly one million years ago. Hot springs. June-Oct. Campground, fishing, pack and saddle trips.

FORT POINT NATIONAL HISTORIC SITE, San Francisco, CA 94129. Built at the entrance to the San Francisco Bay during the years before the Civil War, Fort Point is the largest brick and granite fortification on the west coast of North America. The Golden Gate Bridge looms immediately above the fort.

GOLDEN GATE NATIONAL RECREATION AREA, San Francisco, CA 94123. Large urban park wraps around the west shore of San Francisco and extends north into Marin County. Redwood forests and gentle rolling hills combine with beaches and urban scenery to bring a variety of outdoor recreation opportunities within easy reach of nearby cities.

JOHN MUIR NATIONAL HISTORIC SITE, Martinez, CA 94553. Home of conservationist John Muir, who was instrumental in establishing Yosemite, Mount Rainier, and other national parks.

JOSHUA TREE NATIONAL MONUMENT, Twentynine Palms, CA 92277. Desert preserve with magnificent examples of Joshua tree, cholla cactus, and granite formations. A great variety of desert plants and animals, including the desert bighorn sheep. Campgrounds.

LAVA BEDS NATIONAL MONUMENT, Tulelake, CA 96134. Volcanic formations, including ice caves, lava tubes, and cinder cones, used as a natural fortress by Indians in the Modoc Indian War, 1872-3. Campground, museum.

MUIR WOODS NATIONAL MONUMENT, Mill Valley, CA 94941. Superb stand of virgin redwoods named for conservationist John Muir. Snack bar.

PINNACLES NATIONAL MONUMENT, Paicines, CA 95043. Spires of rock 500 to 1200 feet high combine with caves and other volcanic formations at the monument, in sharp contrast to the smooth terrain of the surrounding country. Campgrounds, rock climbing.

POINT REYES NATIONAL SEASHORE, Point Reyes, CA 94956. Miles of unspoiled beaches backed by tall cliffs follow the coast of this peninsula; forested ridges and upland meadows provide excellent ocean views. Offshore are bird and sea lion communities; gray whales migrate Dec.-Feb. Hike-in campgrounds, snack bar, swimming, fishing.

SANTA MONICA MOUNTAINS NATIONAL RECREATION AREA, Woodland Hills, CA 91364. Stretching 47 miles along the coast west of Los Angeles, this recreation area offers beaches, canyons, and highlands close to the urban millions of Southern California. Campgrounds at state parks within the NRA.

WHISKEYTOWN-SHASTA-TRINITY NATIONAL RECREATION AREA, Whiskeytown, CA 96095. Mountain scenery, water sports, and hiking trails come together in the regions surrounding Whiskeytown Lake. Campgrounds, fishing, boating, water-skiing, swimming.

SOUTHWEST

AZTEC RUINS NATIONAL MONUMENT, Aztec, NM 87410. Ruins of a 12th century town constructed of masonry and timber that was once inhabited by a large community of Pueblo Indians. Museum.

BANDELIER NATIONAL MONUMENT, Los Alamos, NM 87544. Cliff house and pueblo ruins of 15th-century Pueblo Indians are set amidst awesome canyons. Campgrounds, a museum, meals.

CANYON DE CHELLY NATIONAL MONUMENT, Chinle, AZ 86503. Ruins of prehistoric Indian villages are set below sheer red cliffs and in canyon wall caves. Rim drives overlook the ruins; guided tours only into the canyon. Modern Navajo Indians live nearby. Campground, motel, meals, fuel.

CAPULIN MOUNTAIN NATIONAL MONUMENT, Capulin, NM 88414. Crater of extinct but geologically recent volcano rises 1300 feet above the surrounding plain.

CASA GRANDE RUINS NATIONAL MONUMENT, Coolidge, AZ 85228. Massive four-story building constructed 600 years ago stands among ruined walls of prehistoric village. Built of high-lime desert soils, the structure is more typical of construction in prehistoric villages in Mexico than of similar buildings in Arizona. Museum, guided trips.

CEDAR BREAKS NATIONAL MONUMENT, Cedar City, UT 84720. Huge multicolored amphitheater has eroded into the 2,000-foot thick pink cliffs of the Wasatch Formation. June-Oct. Museum, group camp.

Chaco Canyon National Monument, Bloomfield, NM 87413. Prehistoric ruins of 13 major pueblos and hundreds of smaller sites represent a pinnacle of pre-Columbian Pueblo civilization. Approach roads impassable in wet weather. Campground.

Chiricahua National Monument, Willcox, AZ 85643. Strange rock shapes and strata found here were created by volcanic eruptions millions of years ago, then weathered and changed by erosion. Campground; shuttle service to hiking areas.

Coronado National Memorial, Hereford, AZ 85615. Memorial to Spanish explorer Francisco Vasquez de Coronado, who made the first major European exploration of the Southwest in 1540. Located near the site where Coronado entered what is now the United States, the memorial offers an expansive view of his route.

Dinosaur National Monument, Dinosaur, CO 81610. Rich skeletal deposits of prehistoric reptiles are excavated and displayed at Dinosaur Quarry. Rugged back country offers rivers and roads for exploring from May to Oct.; unpaved roads are impassable when wet. Campgrounds, guided river trips.

El Morro National Monument, Ramah, NM 87321. "Inscription Rock" has hundreds of inscriptions by Spanish settlers and American emigrants. Ruins of a 13th century Indian pueblo and petroglyphs are also found within the monument boundaries. Campground, museum.

Fort Bowie National Historic Site, Bowie, AZ 85605. Built in 1862 to secure the entrance to strategic Apache Pass, Fort Bowie served as headquarters for several military campaigns, including operations against Geronimo. Ruins can only be reached along a 1½-mile hiking trail.

Fort Union National Monument, Watrous, NM 87753. A key defensive point on the Santa Fe Trail, three forts were built on this site and occupied between 1851 and 1891. Ruins of the last fort, once the largest military post in the Southwest, have been stabilized.

Gila Cliff Dwellings National Monument, Silver City, NM 88061. Small but well-preserved cliff dwellings were inhabited by prehistoric Indians from about A.D. 100 to 1300. Campgrounds.

Glen Canyon National Recreation Area, Page, AZ 86040. Formed by the Glen Canyon Dam, completed in 1964, Lake Powell stretches 186 miles between Utah and Arizona. Campgrounds, motel, meals, fuel, boating, fishing, water-skiing, swimming, boat tours.

Golden Spike National Historic Site, Brigham City, UT 84302. Site where the Central Pacific and Union Pacific joined tracks in 1869 to complete the first transcontinental railroad in the United States. The meeting is reenacted daily with replicas of the original trains.

Gran Quivira National Monument, Mountainair, NM 87036. Ruins of a 17th-century frontier Spanish mission, built on the site of a prehistoric Indian community. Museum.

Hovenweep National Monument, Mesa Verde National Park, CO 81330. Pueblos, cliff dwellings, and towers were built by Indians before the twelfth century. Six groups of ruins are on the monument grounds; all except Square Tower are difficult to reach. Roads often impassable in wet weather. Campground.

Hubbell Trading Post National Historic Site, Ganado, AZ 86505. Still-active trading post on the Navajo reservation demonstrates the effect of traders on the Indian way of life.

Lake Mead National Recreation Area, Boulder City, NV 89005. Water recreation is the main activity at Lake Mead, formed by Hoover Dam, and Lake Mohave, formed by Davis Dam. Campgrounds, hotels, meals, fuel, boating, swimming, fishing, water-skiing.

Lehman Caves National Monument, Baker, NV 89311. Limestone caverns are decorated by huge stalagmites, stalactites, and other formations. Meals, Apr. to Sept.; guided tours.

Montezuma Castle National Monument, Camp Verde, AZ 86322. This 5-story, 20-room pueblo was built high into limestone cliffs during the twelfth century. It's still 90 percent intact. Montezuma Well, water source for prehistoric Indians, is located at a detached site nearby.

Natural Bridges National Monument, Moab, UT 84532. Three natural sandstone bridges carved by erosion; the largest is 220 feet high, with a span of 268 feet. Roads are sometimes impassable in wet weather. Campground.

Navajo National Monument, Tonalea, AZ 86044. Three of the largest known cliff dwellings—Betatakin, Keet Seel, and Inscription House—are preserved in this monument, located on the Navajo Indian Reservation. Campground; guided horseback tour to Keet Seel.

ORGAN PIPE CACTUS NATIONAL MONUMENT, Ajo, AZ 85321. Plants and wildlife of the Sonoran Desert are preserved in this monument on the Mexican border. Campground.

PECOS NATIONAL MONUMENT, Pecos, NM 87552. Well-preserved ruins of an 18th century mission built over the foundations of a magnificent 17th century church are found at this monument, as are remains of ancient pueblos and kivas.

PIPE SPRING NATIONAL MONUMENT, Moccasin, AZ 86022. Historic 19th century Mormon fort was built by pioneer settlers for protection against hostile Indians. Guided tour.

RAINBOW BRIDGE NATIONAL MONUMENT, Page, AZ 86040. Most massive of world's known natural bridges, this salmon-pink sandstone arch rises 309 feet above the floor of Bridge Canyon. No roads to monument, but concessioners operate boat trips on Lake Powell to arch and flightseeing trips over it.

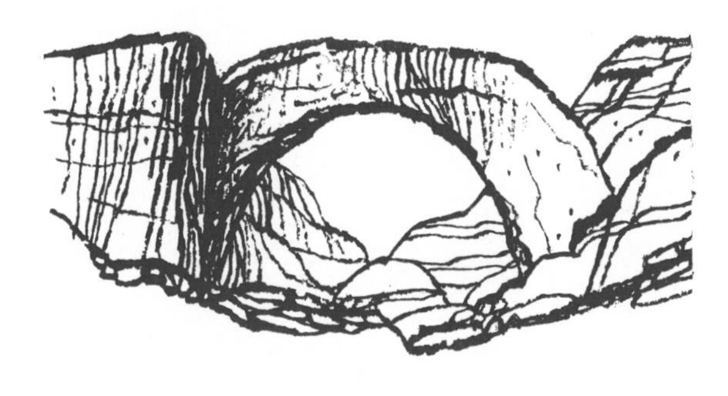

SAGUARO NATIONAL MONUMENT, Tucson, AZ 85731. Multi-branched giant saguaro cacti, unique to the Sonoran desert, reach heights up to 50 feet in this desert preserve. Roads loop through the Tucson Mountain Unit west of Tucson; the Rincon Mountain Unit east of Tucson is primarily designed for hikers, with several primitive campsites along the trails.

SUNSET CRATER NATIONAL MONUMENT, Flagstaff, AZ 86001. Formed by a volcanic eruption in 1064, Sunset Crater is a symmetrical 1,000-foot-high cinder cone. Moisture-retaining ash created by the eruption was important in the development of Indian farming communities in the region, including those preserved at nearby Wupatki National Monument. Entrance road is sometimes closed by snow. Campground.

TIMPANOGOS CAVE NATIONAL MONUMENT, American Fork, UT 84003. Colorful limestone cave is noted for delicate helictite formations that grow in free-form shapes. Cave entrance is a 1½-mile hike from visitor center. May to Oct. Snack bar, guided cave tour.

TONTO NATIONAL MONUMENT, Roosevelt, AZ 85545. Well-preserved 14th century cliff dwellings were built by Salado Indians. Short, steep trail leads to lower ruins; upper ruins are reached along a rigorous 3-mile trail. Make advance arrangements with rangers for guided upper ruins hike.

TUMACACORI NATIONAL MONUMENT, Tumacacori, AZ 85640. Historic 19th century Spanish mission built near a site first visited by Jesuit Father Kino in 1691. Museum.

TUZIGOOT NATIONAL MONUMENT, Clarkdale, AZ 86324. Excavated ruins of a large pueblo that flourished from the 12th to the 15th centuries. Museum.

WALNUT CANYON NATIONAL MONUMENT, Flagstaff, AZ 86001. More than 300 small cliff dwellings built by Sinagua Indians ring 400-foot-deep Walnut Canyon; a ¾-mile trail leads to about 25 of the rooms.

WHITE SANDS NATIONAL MONUMENT, Alamogordo, NM 88310. Sloping dunes of snow-white sand extend for miles; some dunes are 60 feet high. A 16-mile, self-guiding auto trip leads through the monument. Museum, snack bar.

WUPATKI NATIONAL MONUMENT, Flagstaff, AZ 86001. Ruins of red sandstone pueblos built by prehistoric farming Indians; more than 800 pueblos were built in the 56-square-mile area encompassed by the monument. Entrance road from Sunset Crater National Monument sometimes closed by snow. Museum.

ROCKY MOUNTAINS

BENT'S OLD FORT NATIONAL HISTORIC SITE, La Junta, CO 81050. Reconstruction of the trading post operated by Bent, St. Vrain and Company during the mid-19th century and one of the principal trading outlets along the Santa Fe Trail.

BIG HOLE NATIONAL BATTLEFIELD, Wisdom, MT 59761. Site of the 1877 battle between the US Army and Chief Joseph, during his famous retreat to avoid confinement of the Nez Perce Indians to a reservation. Museum.

Bighorn Canyon National Recreation Area, Fort Smith, MT 59035. Scenic Bighorn Lake stretches 71 miles, much of it through rugged, steep-walled Bighorn Canyon. Campgrounds, boating, swimming, fishing, water-skiing, guided tours.

Black Canyon of the Gunnison National Monument, Montrose, CO 81401. Spectacular river gorge is noted for its narrowness, shadowy depth, and vast sheer walls. At points the canyon is 2,700 feet deep, only slightly more than 1,000 feet wide. Late spring to early fall. Campgrounds, meals.

Colorado National Monument, Fruita, CO 81521. Weird rock formations stand amidst sheer-walled canyons up to 2,000 feet deep. A 23-mile rim drive skirts the canyon rim; hiking trails lead into the canyons. Campground.

Craters of the Moon National Monument, Arco, ID 83213. Volcanic phenomena in this lava-covered landscape include cinder cones, craters, lava flows, and ice caves. Campground.

Curecanti National Recreation Area, Gunnison, CO 81230. Water recreation is the main activity in this recreation area, composed of three lakes—Blue Mesa, Morrow Point, and Crystal—that extend 40 miles along the Gunnison River. Campgrounds, boating, fishing, water-skiing, guided boat tours during summer.

Custer Battlefield National Monument, Crow Agency, MT 59022. Site of Custer's famous last stand along the Little Bighorn River in 1876, in which he and 268 soldiers were slain by Indians. Museum and Custer Battlefield National Cemetery are also included at the monument. Guided tours.

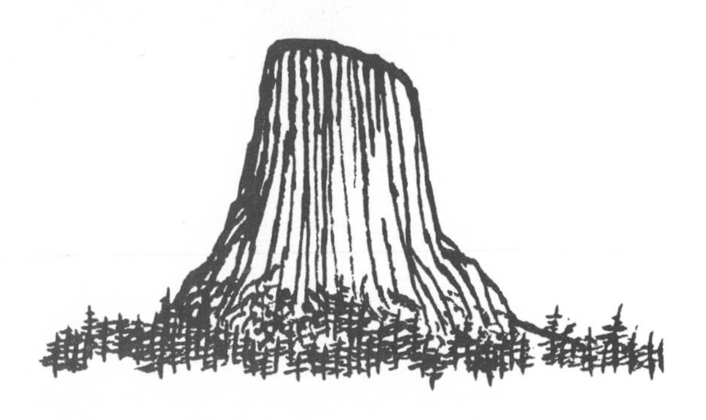

Devils Tower National Monument, Devils Tower, WY 82714. This 865-foot rock pinnacle left by volcanic activity played an important part in Indian folklore. Campground, museum.

Florissant Fossil Beds National Monument, Florissant, CO 80816. More than 80,000 fossilized specimens have been found at this site, including petrified tree stumps, insects, seeds, and leaves. Museum.

Fort Laramie National Historic Site, Fort Laramie, WY 82212. This major military post provided protection for settlers traveling west on the Oregon Trail during the second half of the 19th century. Several buildings have been restored to their original appearance; ruins of others still stand. Museum.

Fossil Butte National Monument, Kemmerer, WY 83101. Rare fish fossils have been preserved for 50 million years here, proving that an ancient sea once covered this semiarid region of western Wyoming. Museum.

Grant-Kohrs Ranch National Historic Site, Deer Lodge, MT 59722. Once one of the largest and best known open range cattle ranches in the country, the Grant-Kohrs Ranch site demonstrates the development of cattle ranching from the mid-19th century through the 1940s. Guided tours.

Great Sand Dunes National Monument, Alamosa, CO 81101. Some of the world's largest sand dunes, reaching heights up to 700 feet. Campground, concessioner-operated back country vehicle tours.

Nez Perce National Historical Park, Spalding, ID 83551. More than 20 different Idaho sites (4 administered by the National Park Service) commemorate the history and culture of the Nez Perce Indians.

ALASKA

With the exception of Glacier Bay and Katmai, few public services are available in Alaska's national monuments. Access to them is usually by chartered bush plane; contact the Alaska Area Office, National Park Service, 540 W. 5th Ave., Anchorage, AK 99501, for information on how to arrange flights.

Aniakchak National Monument, c/o National Park Service, 540 W. 5th Ave., Anchorage, AK 99501. One of the world's largest craters, Aniakchak in southwest Alaska contains a lake, river, and volcano in its 30-square-mile cavity.

Bering Land Bridge National Monument, c/o National Park Service, 540 W. 5th Ave., Anchorage, AK 99501. Only 50 miles from Siberia on the north side of the Seward Peninsula, this promising archeological site contains evidences of the land bridge once connecting Asia and North America.

CAPE KRUSENSTERN NATIONAL MONUMENT, c/o National Park Service, 540 W. 5th Ave., Anchorage, AK 99501. Eskimos have inhabited this Arctic site for 4,000 years; archeological traces of early communities are found in the beach ridges of this Chukchi Sea area.

DENALI NATIONAL MONUMENT, McKinley Park, AK 99755. Adjacent to Mount McKinley National Park, Denali contains the south flank of Mount McKinley and protects caribou, bear, and other wildlife habitats.

GATES OF THE ARCTIC NATIONAL MONUMENT, c/o National Park Service, 540 W. 5th Ave., Anchorage, AK 99501. Vast tundra wilderness amidst the rugged Brooks Range protects habitats of bear, caribou, Dall sheep, and other animals.

GLACIER BAY NATIONAL MONUMENT, Juneau, AK 99802. Massive tidewater glaciers combine with ice-capped mountains and lush forests to create a beautifully remote environment. Concessioner-operated boat trips give excellent views of glaciers. May to Oct. Campground, hotel, meals, marine fuel. Private boating is permitted, but pilot should be experienced with special hazards found at the monument.

KATMAI NATIONAL MONUMENT, King Salmon, AK 99613. The 1912 eruption of Novarupta Volcano created the ash-filled "Valley of Ten Thousand Smokes," where steam rose from fumaroles in the ash. Only a few active vents remain, but the region is still distinguished by volcanic activity, bountiful wildlife, and scenic lakes. Monument is reached only by air, June–Sept. Campground, lodge, tent cabins, meals, fishing.

KENAI FJORDS NATIONAL MONUMENT, c/o National Park Service, 540 W. 5th Ave., Anchorage, AK 99501. This monument on Alaska's southern coast preserves much of the Harding Icefield and the abundant marine life of the Kenai Peninsula fjord system.

KLONDIKE GOLD RUSH NATIONAL HISTORICAL PARK, Skagway, AK 99840. Commemorating the 1898 gold rush, this park preserves historic buildings in Skagway and sections of the Chilkoot and White Pass trails. Limited facilities only in Alaska; orientation center is in Seattle's Pioneer Square area.

KOBUK VALLEY NATIONAL MONUMENT, c/o National Park Service, 540 W. 5th Ave., Anchorage, AK 99501. Set between the Baird and Waring mountains in Alaska's Arctic, the Kobuk River area offers archeological sites, animal habitats, and the Great Kobuk Sand Dunes.

LAKE CLARK NATIONAL MONUMENT, c/o National Park Service, 540 W. 5th Ave., Anchorage, AK 99501. Wildlife abounds in the mountainous terrain encircling Lake Clark, located across the Cook Inlet from Anchorage. Two volcanoes, one of which erupted in 1966, are found in the coastal range. Lodges.

NOATAK NATIONAL MONUMENT, c/o National Park Service, 540 W. 5th Ave., Anchorage, AK 99501. The 65-mile arctic Grand Canyon of the Noatak is the country's largest mountain-ringed basin still unaffected by technology. Prehistoric archeological sites abound.

SITKA NATIONAL HISTORICAL PARK, Sitka, AK 99835. Historic site of 1804 battle between the Tlingit Indians and Russian settlers. Tlingit totem poles are displayed.

WRANGELL-ST. ELIAS NATIONAL MONUMENT, c/o National Park Service, 540 W. 5th Ave., Anchorage, AK 99501. Wilderness monument with more glaciers and peaks than any other site in the country. Includes 18,008-foot Mount St. Elias, the second highest peak in the continent. Rustic lodges.

YUKON-CHARLEY NATIONAL MONUMENT, c/o National Park Service, 540 W. 5th Ave., Anchorage, AK 99501. Long stretches of two scenic rivers—the Yukon and the Charley—are protected, along with the largest nesting concentrations of the endangered peregrine falcon. Rustic lodge.

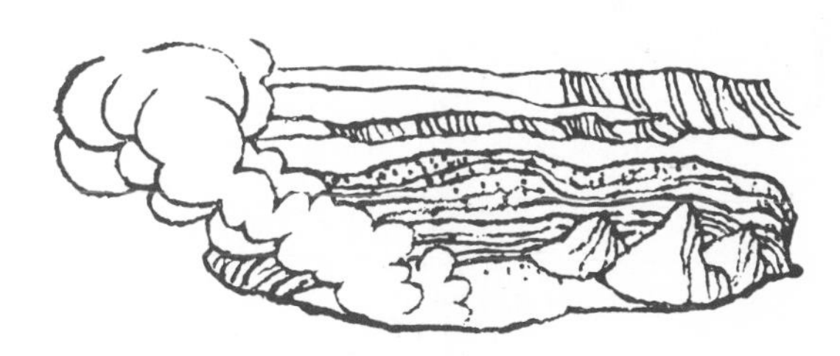

HAWAII

KALOKO-HONOKOHAU NATIONAL HISTORICAL PARK, Honolulu, HI 96850. On the west side of Hawaii Island, park is a Hawaiian cultural center.

PUUHONUA O HONAUNAU NATIONAL HISTORICAL PARK, Honaunau, HI 96726. Prehistoric Hawaiian sanctuary where warriors, noncombatants, and kapu breakers could escape death by reaching sacred ground.

PUUKOHOLA HEIAU NATIONAL HISTORIC SITE, Kawaihae, HI 96743. Ruins of temple built by King Kamehameha the Great during his rise to power.

Index

Abbreviations: **NP,** National Park; **NS,** National Seashore; **NM,** National Monument; **NHS,** National Historic Site; **NHP,** National Historical Park; **NBS,** National Battlefield Site; **NRA,** National Recreation Area; **SP,** State Park.